Contents

46-53 Blue Peter Flies the World

96-97 Bath Spa

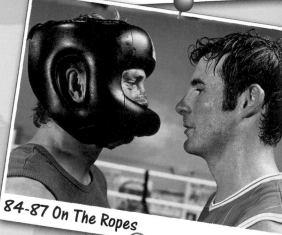

34-37 Now Get Out of That

84-87 On The Ropes

**Written by Richard Marson
and Anne Dixon**

98-101 The Pain of 'P' Company

16-21 Thunderbirds Are Go!

64-67 Christmas is Coming!

90-91 Lederhosen Madness

Blue Peter

BBC

Annual **2005**

Published by Pedigree Books Limited
Beach Hill House, Walnut Gardens, Exeter, Devon, EX4 4DH.
Email: books @pedigreegroup.co.uk
By arrangement with the BBC.

Pedigree®

£7.99

Hello

Welcome to our latest Blue Peter book.

It's exactly 40 years since the very first one appeared and we can't think of many other television programmes which have had a book devoted to them for four decades! Our tip is - hang onto this book. Maybe one day it will be worth over £100 – the current average price for the ultra-rare book one.

With over 120 programmes to choose from, as usual it has been a bit of a headache to cram everything in. As well as some our favourite reports and stories, there are loads of the best makes and cooks. And on this page we have included snapshots from some of the other highlights of the last 12 months – see how many you can remember (the answers are on page 109)

This was the year when Blue Peter entered the record books as the world's longest continuously running children's programme – and we revealed our official Guinness certificate on the day of another first – 12-year-old Blue Peter viewer Ryan Gilpin became the first child ever to present the programme after winning a special competition.

Blue Peter

6

There!

Another wonderful moment was the news that the programme had won the prestigious BAFTA (a bit like the TV Oscars) for Best Factual Programme. On top of that, Matt won the BAFTA as Best Children's Presenter for the second year running. You could be a winner too as we award Blue Peter badges all year round (see page 108 for more details) – and we'd be delighted to hear from you.

The saddest news of the year was the death of dear old George the tortoise. We buried him in a place of honour in the Blue Peter garden and you can read about George's friend and successor Shelley on page 73.

Just as we were about to set off on our summer expedition, Liz told us the great news that she was expecting a baby. Liz is hoping to return to Blue Peter after her baby is born and we'll certainly be keeping you closely in touch with mother and child over the next few months.

All in all it's been a brilliant year but nothing beats the excitement of Blue Peter's new five times a week slot on the CBBC Channel – complete with a brand-new look for our studio and the latest arrangement of our famous signature tune, Barnacle Bill. We'll be there Monday to Friday every single week from September to June – and don't worry if you're not digital yet – because we'll be on CBBC1 every Monday, Wednesday and Friday too.

We hope you enjoy this book and all our new programmes!

Blue Peter

DOH! PLACE

If you want to make a sitting room for your favourite cartoon characters the first thing you will need is an empty grocery box and a clear space to work in.

1. For the room, paint the inside of the grocery box with pink paint or cover with pink paper. For the floor, cover with turquoise paper or fabric.

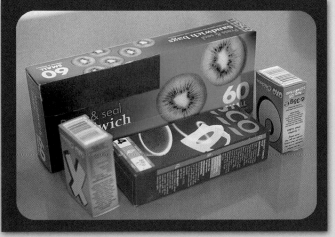

2. The sofa is the most important piece of furniture for the family to sit on. It's made from different sized boxes. We used a small soup box, a sandwich bag box, 2 small stock cube boxes together with a strip of corrugated card, wadding, brown fabric and a needle and thread.

3. Cut the soup box to measure 13 x 5 cm (this will be the seat of the sofa) and cut the bag box to measure 8.5 cm x 18 cm long and reseal the end of the box (this will be the back of the sofa).

LIKE HOME

4. Cut the stock cube boxes to measure 5 cm high – they will become the sides of the sofa. Mark roughly where the stock cube boxes will be on the sofa back and mark and cut a curved section on both ends of the bag box. Cut a length of corrugated card which will reach from one end to the other and stick in place to cover the gaps in the box.

6. The TV is another stock cube box, a mauve drinking straw, matching paint and paper, bits of corrugated cardboard for knobs, silver paint, modelling clay and a hair pin.

Empty and reseal the ends of the stock cube box. Paint it mauve and cut 4 x 6 cm lengths of drinking straw for the legs. Make a hole in each corner of the box and push a length of straw through each one.

5. Wrap each section of the sofa with a layer of wadding or cotton wool and then cover with brown fabric. Stitch around the curves of the arms on the outside and then join the sofa back, seat and sides together.

7. Cut out a picture from a magazine and glue in place. Cut 2 circles and 1 oblong from corrugated card. Paint them silver and stick to one side of the screen for TV control knobs.

For the video or DVD player which sits on top of the TV, cut down a small box to fit on top. Roll a piece of modelling clay into a small ball and stick a hair pin into it and press on top.

Blue Peter

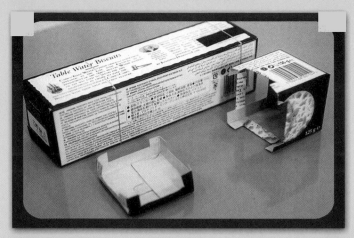

8. For the telephone table you will need another box. A square cracker box is ideal plus wood effect sticky-backed plastic or brown paint and a few more pieces of card.

Cut two sections from the ends of the cracker box – one measuring 6 cm and the other 2 cm. Reseal the ends on both sections. Shape the two sections by cutting out the middles roughly 1 cm from the cut edge. Do this on all four sides. On the larger piece of the box also cut a hole on one of the sides. Paint them brown or cover the outsides with sticky-backed plastic for a realistic wood effect.

Push the small section inside the large one so that the legs line up. The sealed end of the small section becomes a shelf. Tape the two together underneath. Cut a piece of card exactly the same size as the top of the unit, cover with a lighter brown sticky-backed plastic. Make some books from pieces of thick card.

9. The table lamp is a small plastic bottle top covered with red and green tape. Cut out a curved shape in purple card and bend it to form a lampshade. Glue the ends when you are happy with the shape. Press modelling clay on top of the lid and push a short length of straw into it.

Cut a small circle of card and make small snips all the way around it. Bend in the edges and attach it to the top of the straw with modelling clay. The shade should rest on top of the card circle.

10. The standard lamp is made from 2 mauve bendy drinking straws, a lump of modelling clay, a small paper cake or chocolate case and a bottle top.

Stretch out the bendy sections on both straws. Keep one full length and cut down the second straw 1 cm either side of the bendy section. Push the small section into the long straw at the bendy end. Glue in place and allow to dry.

Make a hole in the centre of chocolate case, push the small straw through and glue in place. If you can find a small plastic bead, glue this in the middle for a light bulb.

Press modelling clay into a bottle top and stand the long straw in it.

11. The magazine rack is also made from card and sticky-backed plastic. Cut 2 shapes as shown from thin card. These will be the ends of the magazine rack. Cut 2 more slightly longer pieces of card as shown and cover all 4 sections with sticky-backed plastic. Attach all 4 sections together with glue or leftover scraps of sticky-backed plastic.

Draw around the base on thin card and cut out. Attach it to the rack with glue and fill with tiny sections of folded pieces of comics or magazines.

12. Home comforts – the rug is a series of different coloured oval shapes cut from felt. Glue one on top of the other.

The plant pot is the top section of a plastic drinks bottle. Cut from under the screw section roughly 6 cm down. Paint the inside and leave to dry. Fill with modelling clay. The leaves are cut from crepe paper or card and glued onto a long green pipe cleaner. Push the stem into the modelling clay and stand in an upturned lid.

The wall hanging plant is two pen lids decorated with permanent marker. Scrunch up some tissue paper and glue between the two open ends before attaching to the wall.

The picture is a rectangle of card 12 x 8 cm covered with pale blue paper. Glue a darker blue strip along one of the long sides. Cut out shapes from red and white card to make a ship and clouds. Stick strips of brown card around the edge to look like a frame. Tape some string on the back of the picture and use a map pin to attach to the sitting room wall.

Blue Peter

CHANGING

The ceremony of the changing of the guard at Buckingham Palace is one of Britain's most popular tourist attractions. It happens every 24 or 48 hours depending on the time of year – and it always draws a large crowd.

Behind the scenes, a lot of very hard work goes into making the ceremony look as smart and impressive as it does – as I found out when I reported to Chelsea Barracks in London, home to number 7 company Coldstream Guards – the soldiers in charge. Although there was no way they were going to let a civilian like me loose on the forecourt of Buckingham Palace itself, they had agreed to let me take part in the all-important check parade the guards must undergo before they can perform the ceremony.

Before that, I had to learn how to drill like a real guardsman.

First I changed into uniform, which at least helped make me look and feel the part. The drill training itself took a lot of concentration. Drill is made up of a whole series of sharply executed moves which must be performed by every soldier on parade at precisely the same moment. You must react to a command instantly and I soon became used to the noise of everybody's boots crashing onto the parade square in unison as we were put through our paces. There is absolutely no room for error – and, as I discovered, no allowance made for Blue Peter presenters either! All the time I was out on the parade square I felt the eagle eyes of the CSM – or Company Sergeant Major – boring into me to spot any mistakes. Luckily, I seemed to do ok.

THE GUARD

The check parade over, I'd passed muster and really enjoyed myself. Now the guards were off to get ready for the actual ceremony. I changed too – back into civvies – to rush up to Buckingham Palace where I was allowed a prime view of the proceedings. Overall, the changing of the guard only lasts 45 minutes. But as I watched this ancient ceremony in full swing, I had a new respect for the hard graft which goes into the making of such an impressive military spectacle.

Once I'd passed the drill training, I was allowed to take part in the check parade – on the morning of the actual changing of the guard. This meant I got to wear the famous busby – the tall furry hat famous throughout the world. It weighs an absolute tonne and one of the guardsmen told me that in the heat of summer, combined with a tight, high-necked parade uniform, it is not unheard-of for a soldier to faint on parade.

The check parade line-up is another exercise in military precision. I had to find my place in the line, smallest to the left, tallest to the right – with me ending up somewhere in the middle. It seemed to go well – I concentrated like mad and didn't bring any shame on the honour of Blue Peter!

a JUMBO

Up in the Blue Peter office, there's a complicated set of charts, known as 'the sheets' which cover each day of the year. Our film team use these sheets to plan every detail of the presenters' schedules, so when I'm in the office I often sneak a look to see what stories are in the pipeline. They're all given a title and I must say I raised an eyebrow when I read 'babysitting' as a film report with my name next to it. Not a very typical Blue Peter story, I thought. But then, as I soon discovered, this was babysitting with a difference because the baby in question was a two-week-old Asian elephant!

She'd been born in Whipsnade Wild Animal Park and before I was allowed to meet her, I had to prove I was up to the job of working with elephants. Above all (and just as with human babysitters), it was essential that the baby's parents, mum Kaylee and dad Emmett, were comfortable with me around.

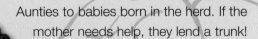

My feet didn't touch the ground – I slogged away, doing all the chores from mucking out (basically that's clearing up the elephant poo – and there's always lots of it), to helping to scrub down the baby's Auntie – Lyang-Lyang. One of the keepers explained that Lyang-Lyang isn't really the baby's Auntie but she's known as that because in the wild all female elephants act as Aunties to babies born in the herd. If the mother needs help, they lend a trunk!

In the wild, elephants rub up against rocks or trees to remove dead skin but at Whipsnade every elephant gets a full body scrub. It was obvious that Lyang-Lyang enjoyed every minute of her pampering but to me, it felt very like scrubbing a kitchen floor!

sized baby

At last I was allowed to get close to my charge and it was a magical moment. We went for a walk in the spring sun – and although she was still only two weeks old, she was already an impressive size. Actually, she's thought to be the heaviest baby elephant ever born in captivity, weighing the same as two adult men. As I quickly discovered, she loves a roll in the dirt!

Elephants are pregnant for 21 months so the bond between a baby and its mum is very strong indeed. In fact, throughout the day Mum was never far away, so truthfully I didn't really do much of a job as a babysitter. But I didn't mind at all. It was enough to help out and get this close to such a wonderful group of animals.

Peter

Worldwide, only about 40,000 Asian elephants survive today and so I really hope that the newest arrival in Whipsnade's breeding programme will help the conservation effort to save this magnificent but endangered species.

P.S. – If you'd like to take a look at Whipsnade's elephants and you're a Blue Peter badge winner, you can get in free!

THUNDERBIRDS
ARE GO!

It was a hit TV show in the 1960s and it was a summer smash movie in 2004. So if you'd like to create your very own Tracy Island you will need the following:

- Large grocery carton
- Sandpaper
- Cereal packet for cardboard
- 2 medium and 1 small matchbox
- Newspapers
- Foam Sponge
- Kitchen foil
- Drinking straw
- PVA glue
- Corrugated cardboard
- Soap powder packet
- Brass paper fastener
- Oblong cheese box

- Pipe cleaners
- Paper bowl
- Green, brown and blue paper
- 2 washing-up liquid bottles
- Matt paint in green, brown and grey
- Small adhesive labels
- Sawdust
- 75mm flower pot saucer
- Sticky tape

Blue Peter

Base

Using the side of a strong grocery carton, draw a rough rectangular shape (about 35cm x 50cm) with three rounded corners and the fourth jutting out to allow for Thunderbird 2's runway.

Cut it out.

Thunderbird 2 Hangar

Cut away the flaps at one end of a soap powder packet. Cut away the other end at a sloping angle so that it will fit the back of the base facing the runway. Fix the packet to the base with strips of sticky tape. The building on top of the hangar is a cream cheese box painted grey. Fix just the back edge of this box to the hangar with sticky tape overlapping the hangar front by about 3cm. The box should not be fixed at the front, as the hangar door will slide under it later. Keep the cheese box lid to use as part of the house at a later stage. Use part of a paper bowl for the curved roof. To get the right shape first cut off the outer rim then cut the remaining piece in half. Paint grey. Secure the corners of the roof to the sides of the building with sticky tape.

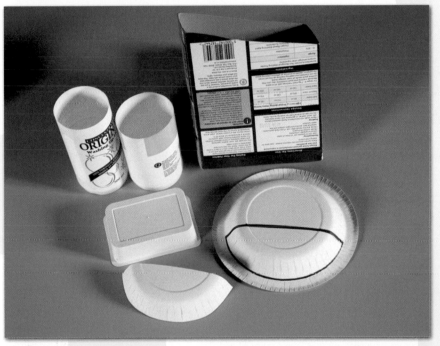

Thunderbird 1 and 3 Launch Pads

These are made from washing-up liquid bottles. For Thunderbird 1 cut the bottle down to about 12cm in height. Fix to the middle of the base with sticky tape. Cut the bottle for Thunderbird 3 to about 14cm in height. Fix to base near remaining front corner with sticky tape.

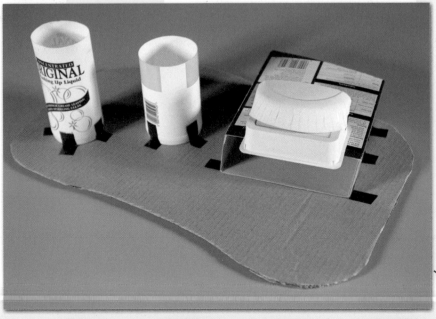

The Landscape

The shape of the island is built up from crumpled newspaper spread with PVA glue. Thin the glue down with water to make it go further, then brush the glue on a half sheet of newspaper. Crumple the paper then press it onto the base with more glue. Don't use too much – just enough to hold the paper in place. Leave spaces for a beach at the front and a small cave at the back. Build up the landscape to the height of the tub in the middle and leave a few centimetres below the top of the second tub uncovered. The areas around the tubs should be fairly flat, as should the space at the back where the house will be placed. Completely cover the soap powder packet except for the ends. Pile up paper over the building and roof and some more at the back for hills.

Finish off by gluing on strips of paper overlapping each other to hold the whole thing together. Leave the base somewhere warm to dry. The base should feel quite light when it is dry. You could make the house and trees whilst waiting for the base.

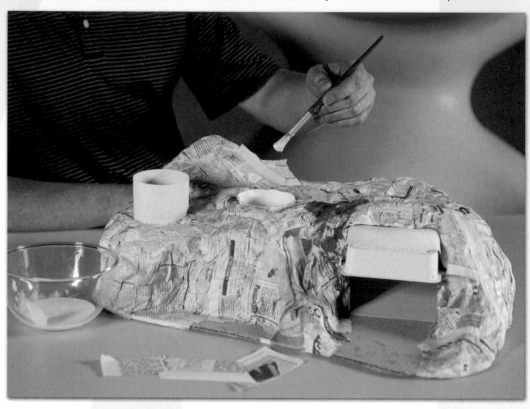

 When the base is completely dry, paint the cliffs brown and the top green. If you add some sawdust to the green paint it will give a grassy look. Paint the outside of the Thunderbird 3 launch pad tub grey. When all the painted parts are dry, glue a piece of sandpaper on the beach area and inside the bottom of the cave.

6 The windows on Thunderbird 2's runway building are blue self-adhesive labels. You could easily colour white ones. Cut the labels off in a strip to fit the front of the building, leave on the backing and glue them in place.

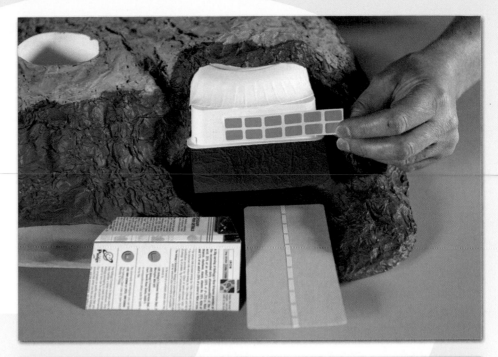

7 The hangar door is a rectangle of cereal packet cardboard covered in kitchen foil. Paint it brown to match the cliffs. It should fit the hangar front with an extra flap that can be bent over at the top and then pushed into the space between the hangar and the building – the door can then slide up and down when Thunderbird 2 is ready to launch.

Thunderbird 2 Runway

8 Cut out a rectangle of stiff card and paint it grey. Make markings down the centre from strips cut from sticky labels. Glue the runway onto the base in front of the hangar.

Swimming Pool

9 Cut out a piece of cereal packet that will fit over the centre tube and overlap it all round. Cut a hole in the middle to allow Thunderbird 1 to lift off. Cut out a rim for the pool a little larger than the opening, cover both pieces with kitchen foil to give texture and then paint them grey. When the paint is dry, glue a piece of blue card or paper under the rim. Fix the two layers together with a small brass paper fastener. This will allow the swimming pool to slide to one side for lift off. Glue the pool in place over the centre tub. Stuff the bottom of the tub with paper so that the tip of Thunderbird 1 is just beneath pool level.

Observation Tower above Thunderbird 3 Launch Pad

Cut out another piece of cereal packet to fit over the tub, cover with foil and paint grey to match the swimming pool surround. The circular building at the top is made from a flower pot saucer.

Cut a hole in the bottom the size of the tub opening. Glue the top edge of the saucer to a ring of card that also has the tub-sized hole cut out of it. Paint grey, fix on blue labels for windows then fit it over the tub edge. Stuff with paper so that Thunderbird 3 shows just above the tower top.

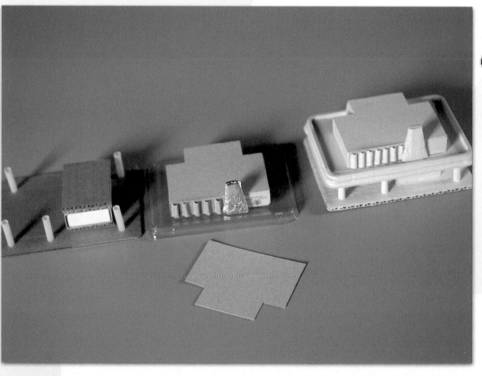

The House

The main building on the upper storey is made from a medium sized matchbox with a section from a second box taped at the back. Make a chimney from two layers of thick card, cover with foil for texture, then glue to the long side of the complete matchbox. Glue a strip of corrugated cardboard by the side of the chimney. Cover the tops of the boxes with a piece of card to cover the join. Glue the buildings to the lid from the cheese box.

The lower floor of this building is a small matchbox with some layers of cardboard glued on to make it higher. Glue onto a base made from a piece of thick card the same size as the cheese box lid. Paint the two sections grey then glue them on top of each other with pieces of drinking straw in between them for pillars. Fix the house on the flat area behind the swimming pool.

Steps

Cut a small strip of corrugated card to form steps between the house and the swimming pool and another to link the observation tower to the pool. Paint the steps grey and glue in position.

Trees and Bushes

The palm tree trunks are pipe cleaners cut in half with brown paper wrapped around them. Cut out strips of green paper and shape into leaves

and glue around the top of the trunks. Spread out the tips of the leaves so they look realistic. Make small holes with the tip of a pencil at each side of the runway then push the end of the tree trunks into them. The trees disguise the runway and can be pushed aside for launching Thunderbird 2. Fix more trees on the green area of the island. Make a few bunches of leaves for plants and some bushes from scraps of foam sponge coloured green. When fixed in place they can be very useful for covering up any torn or bare parts.

This is the most popular make in the history of Blue Peter!
We hope you'll enjoy making it

Blue Peter

Get Together

All over the UK there are thousands of clubs catering for all sorts of activities like swimming, judo, gymnastics, dancing, football and tennis. If you want to join a club, you simply go along, sign up and do the things you love as well as making new friends.

Unfortunately that's not the case for a whole group of children who miss out on these opportunities because they have a learning disability.

In Britain alone, over 200 babies are born every week with learning disabilities. We heard that the charity Mencap wanted to set up a training programme for volunteer helpers to go to clubs and help children with a learning disability.

The cost of setting up the scheme and training nearly 3,000 volunteers was £500,000 but this extra support would go on for years and years into the future. We felt sure Blue Peter viewers would want to get together and help.

Bring and buy sales were the answer and in a matter of weeks we sent out over 15,000 kits. The Blue Peter Get Together Appeal really took off and news of sales happening in all four corners of the UK reached us.

Eleven-year-old Jessica Hemming from Aylesbury wrote to tell us how pleased she was that we were helping children with special needs as her sister Samantha has Downs Syndrome. Together they ran a sale in their dining room and raised £61.

Kitty, Nicola and Nellie raised £233.86 at Kings Nympton School in Devon. They said they had a great time and their classroom was packed with stalls.

Bring & Buy Sale
Top tips on how to organise your Sale

Blue Peter Get Together
MENCAP

Appeal

Class 7RS at Oxford Community School organised a cake sale and sent a photo of themselves after they had counted up their takings which came to £52.84!

Apart from selling home made cakes and cups of tea, aromatherapy massage was on offer at St Albans Church in Streatham. Daisy, Laura, Emma, Avni, Charlotte, Rose and Sasha organised the sale raising £184 thanks to lots of encouragement and support from their local community.

Laurie and Christian Denman from the 20th Royal Tunbridge Wells Scout Group organised a successful sale which resulted in a grand total of £103.28.

Catherine, Georgina and Grace from the 38th Leeds Brownies held a raffle and bun sale and sent £58 for the appeal.

Laura, Daniel and Becky visited us in the studio. Because of your hard work they are just three children with a learning disability who are now going to out of school clubs and fully taking part thanks to extra support from volunteers whose special training has been paid for by our Get Together Appeal.

Blue Peter viewers everywhere really did get together and smashed our appeal target of £500,000. By the summer of 2004, the amount you raised was just under three quarters of a million pounds. THANK YOU.

Blue Peter

23

I'd only just woken up when I took the call from the Blue Peter office. "Morning Konnie", said a cheery voice at the end of the 'phone. "Listen we want you to change a lightbulb."

Don't

I muttered something under my breath. "Can't you change it yourself?"

"Ah, but it's no ordinary kind of lightbulb" went on the cheery voice, "it's 150 metres up…."

The lightbulb in question was one of the aircraft warning lights fitted at the top of the Forth Road Bridge near Edinburgh in Scotland to stop planes from crashing into the towering structure. A few days later I found myself at the base of the bridge, dressed in a thick boiler suit to protect myself from the icy wind. It was a good suit too because I didn't feel the cold – the problem was that the wind was so strong, I was having trouble standing upright. I could only imagine what it would feel like right at the top….

A lift takes you part of the way there but for what seemed like miles, the only way up was by climbing a long series of vertical iron ladders. Once I made it outside, I momentarily forgot my fears about the high winds because the view was just breathtaking. Then, slowly but surely, I made my way over to the highest point where the warning light was waiting for its new bulb.

LOOK DOWN

Really it was a pretty simple operation – but I was very glad I don't have a fear of heights. From where I was standing, the cars below looked ridiculously tiny. "Little do they know…" I thought.

The Forth Road Bridge has been a vital traffic link for people travelling in and out of Edinburgh ever since it opened in 1964. It's one of the largest suspension bridges in Europe and as well as routine maintenance – like changing the lightbulb – a team of workers labour on the bridge all year round to keep it in tip top shape.

My mind wandered back to that cheery voice from the Blue Peter office. "I've done it", I smiled, "but next time they call I might just leave my 'phone on voicemail…"

Be My

Blue Peter

Gather together the following materials:

- cardboard tube
- card from a cereal packet
- coloured card
- wrapping paper or fabric
- 2 bottle tops filled with modelling clay
- a length of narrow and wide ribbon
- scraps of paper
- Stickers or sequins
- glue and sticky tape

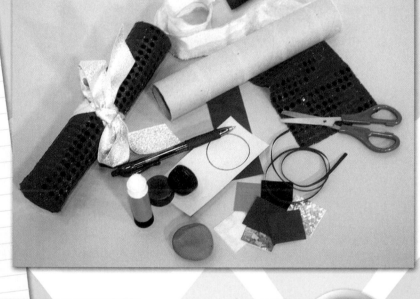

1

Cut the cardboard tube in half. Cut a strip of coloured card roughly 14 x 4 cm. Bend this strip into a circle and fit it inside one half of the tube. Glue in place leaving about 3 cm sticking out.

Valentine...

2

Cut a length of narrow ribbon long enough to stretch the length of both tubes plus enough for your message. Use sticky tape to fix one end of the ribbon to the outside of one tube and then thread it through. Pass the ribbon through the second tube and tape it to the outside as before.

3

Using the end of the tube as a pattern, draw around it twice on a cereal packet and cut out 2 circles.

To cover the cardboard circles, cut 2 more slightly larger circles in fabric or coloured paper. Glue the card circles on top of these. Using scissors, carefully snip around the edges as far as the cardboard.

To ensure the tubes stand up and display your message, fill 2 bottle tops with modelling clay and glue them in the middle of the cardboard circles.

Brush some glue onto the tabs and attach one circle on each of the cardboard tubes. To match the covered ends, cut 2 pieces of fabric or paper to cover each tube. Glue in place.

Blue Peter

Now for the all important message. Cut out small squares from coloured card. They must be small enough to fit inside the tube. Then cut out hearts and letters to spell out your message. Ideally you need two sets of letters so the message can be read from both sides. Stick them onto the squares and then attach them to the ribbon.

4

5

Fold up the squares and put them inside the tube. Push the two tubes together and for a finishing touch, tie a wide ribbon in a bow around the middle. Your sweetheart is bound to love it!

You could adapt this idea for all sorts of special occasions.

Blue Peter

BUSTED ON B.P.

Charlie, James and Mattie – the boys from Busted – made one of their first ever tv appearances on Blue Peter. That was way back in November 2002 but since then they've become really good friends of the programme. They've already scored a triple platinum first album and a whole series of top five hits including the theme from the Thunderbirds movie.

On this occasion, they were in the studio to help us tell the noisy story of the classic Stratocaster guitar – and both Simon and Matt had a go. I think my expression says it all – I told them to leave it to the experts – which was the perfect cue for Busted to blast into their latest pop rock anthem!

Blue Peter

Dear Blue

Keep those letters and photos coming. We love hearing from you and seeing your pictures. Apart from the possiblity they may be shown on TV there's a very good chance they'll earn you a badge!

You'll become part of our huge family of badge winners and, as an added bonus, wearing one entitles you to free entry at over 200 attractions. We'll send you a list of all these places with your badge.

Here are a few viewers who have put pen to paper and won themselves Blue Peter badges.

I am writing to express a wish concerning the letter P in your Blue Peter Dogs Alphabet. My dog is a Pinscher and it would be nice to see the breed on your show.
Yours
Laura Ward
Eastleigh, Hampshire

We thought we'd send you a photo of us with our auntie's tortoise. He is called Billy. We looked after him while she was on holiday and really enjoyed it.
Love from
Lucy and Connor Cartwright
Stourbridge, West Midlands

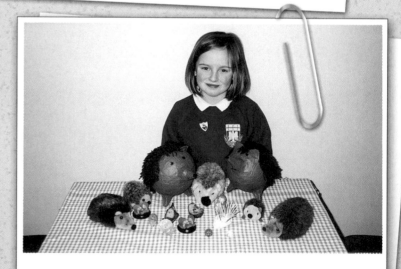

I made these hedgehog money boxes using the information from the Blue Peter website. I am already saving up in mine. Hedgehogs are my favourite animal and I have a collection of them.
Love from
Ruth Augarde
Durham

Peter

I enclose a photo of me and your Mother's Day flower card make which I finished by 6 pm Monday night. I am giving it on Sunday to my Grandma. Is this a record time for completing one of your makes?
Love
Daniel Randell
Bristol

I had a clear out of my bedroom and I came across loads of things to recycle, such as my old magazines. This is a picture of me dropping them into my blue bin to be recycled. MORE PEOPLE SHOULD RECYCLE!
Love
Kirsty Redman
Poulton-Le-Fylde

I like watching the Dogs Alphabet. This is a picture of me and my dog Sam. He likes running, bouncing and playing. He is a mongrel so he could be the letter M.
Love
Mark Ward
Chesterfield

Thank you for inspiring me with your pudding for Burns Night. As it was my sister's 15th birthday I decided to make Crannachan as a surprise. It was delicious!!
Best Wishes
Kate Highy
Windsor

Matty's

Ingredients:

200 g digestive biscuits

100 g unsalted butter

200 g marshmallows

2 tbsp milk

2 tsp coffee granules dissolved in 2 tbsp water

200 g chocolate

200 ml double cream

1. Put the biscuits into a plastic bag and crush them with a rolling pin.

2. Melt the butter over a low heat and add it to the crushed biscuits. Stir well.

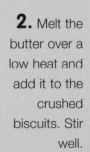

3. A flan tin with a loose bottom is ideal for this pie. Line it with the biscuit mixture and press down until it is flat. Put it in the fridge for around 30 minutes.

Mud Pies

4. Break the chocolate into small pieces. Put it in a bowl and carefully rest it inside a larger bowl containing enough boiling water to cover the bottom of the smaller bowl. The chocolate should melt quite quickly.

5. Remove the melted chocolate and fold in the double cream.

6. For the topping, put the milk and coffee into a small saucepan. Add the marshmallows and melt over a low heat, keep stirring as you don't want this to burn and then gently fold into the chocolate and cream.

7. Remove the pie base from the fridge and pour the topping over it. Put the pie back in the fridge for between 2 to 3 hours before serving.

Matt used a 24 cm cake tin which made 8 slices of Mud Pie.

If you have individual pie tins, you could make small versions.

NOW GET

Meet 16-year-old Blue Peter viewer Tom Lyon. When other boys his age were asking for bikes and video games for Christmas and birthdays, Tom wanted handcuffs and strait-jackets. That's because he's been fascinated by escapology – the art of escaping from ropes, chains and straps – ever since he can remember, and soon after Tom first emailed us to tell us about his hobby, he came to the Blue Peter studio to show just how good he was.

That was back in 2001. More recently, Tom set Simon a challenge. He suggested that both Simon and himself be tightly strapped into regulation hospital strait-jackets – used to restrain violent patients – with just two minutes to escape. While Simon would be free to move about as he wished, Tom would also be suspended upside down from our studio roof.

OUT OF THAT!

Simon lost no time in accepting the challenge – more out of curiosity than anything else. As Blue Peter went live, everyone in the studio felt nervous – but just a couple of minutes into the programme Tom had triumphed. He was free – but meanwhile on the floor, Simon was still sweating and struggling away, securely trapped in his jacket. Matt took pity on him and let him out but Simon still felt it was a case of unfinished business.

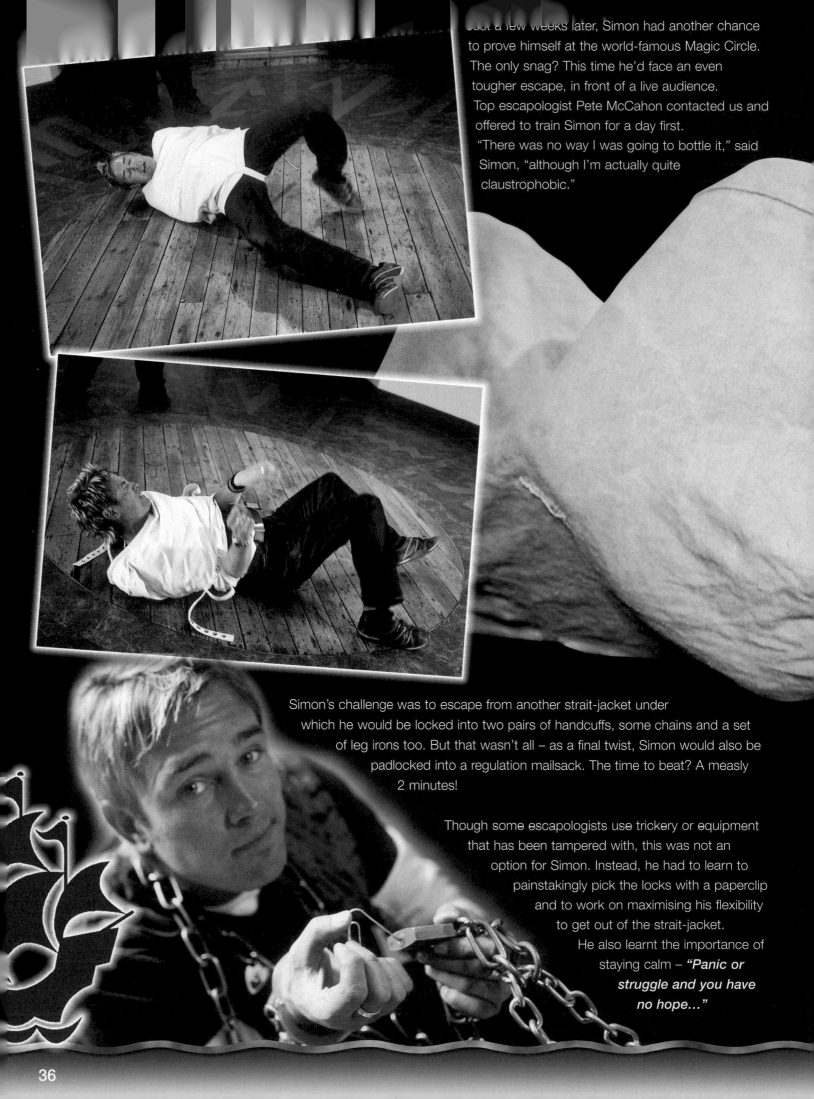

Just a few weeks later, Simon had another chance to prove himself at the world-famous Magic Circle. The only snag? This time he'd face an even tougher escape, in front of a live audience.

Top escapologist Pete McCahon contacted us and offered to train Simon for a day first.

"There was no way I was going to bottle it," said Simon, "although I'm actually quite claustrophobic."

Simon's challenge was to escape from another strait-jacket under which he would be locked into two pairs of handcuffs, some chains and a set of leg irons too. But that wasn't all – as a final twist, Simon would also be padlocked into a regulation mailsack. The time to beat? A measly 2 minutes!

Though some escapologists use trickery or equipment that has been tampered with, this was not an option for Simon. Instead, he had to learn to painstakingly pick the locks with a paperclip and to work on maximising his flexibility to get out of the strait-jacket.

He also learnt the importance of staying calm – *"Panic or struggle and you have no hope..."*

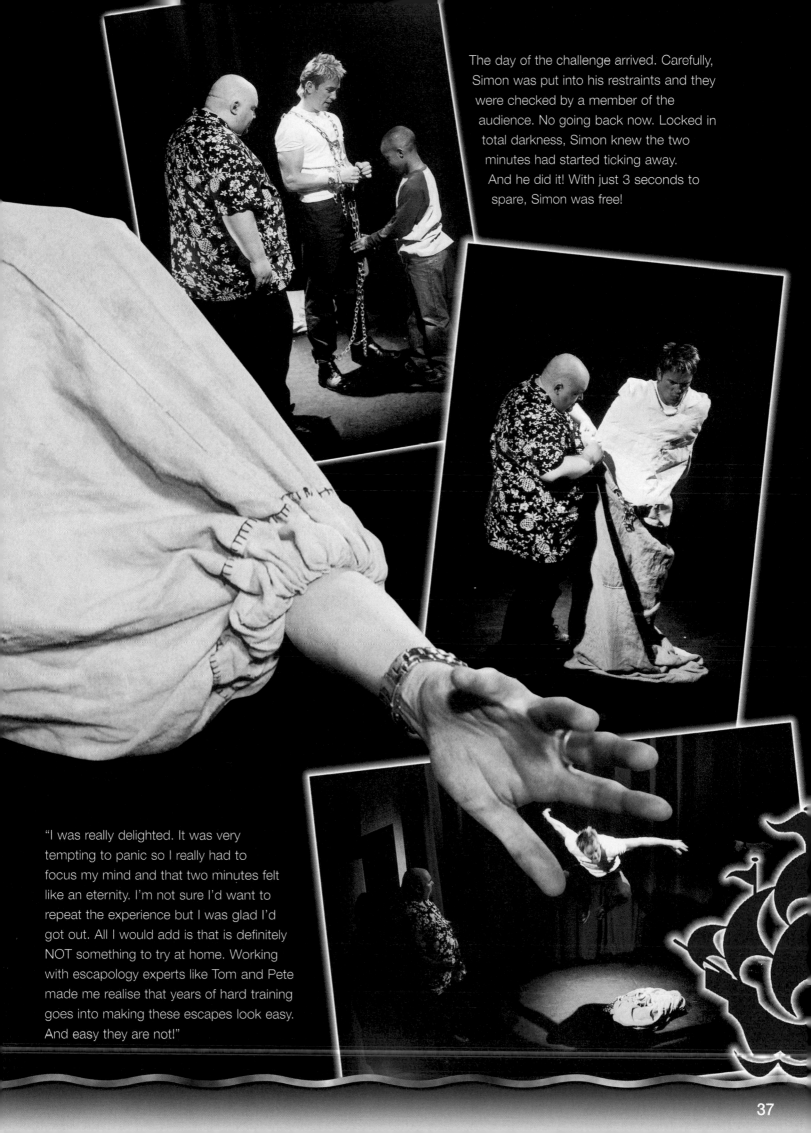

The day of the challenge arrived. Carefully, Simon was put into his restraints and they were checked by a member of the audience. No going back now. Locked in total darkness, Simon knew the two minutes had started ticking away. And he did it! With just 3 seconds to spare, Simon was free!

"I was really delighted. It was very tempting to panic so I really had to focus my mind and that two minutes felt like an eternity. I'm not sure I'd want to repeat the experience but I was glad I'd got out. All I would add is that is definitely NOT something to try at home. Working with escapology experts like Tom and Pete made me realise that years of hard training goes into making these escapes look easy. And easy they are not!"

Blue Peter

Simon **Thomas**

"For me, Blue Peter is a dream job – and I never forget how lucky I am. Mind you, it took me several attempts to get the job so when I did, I was really ready for it. My motto in life is to go for it – luck plays a part of course but if you really want something and you work for it, I reckon that's the best way to achieve your dreams.

Ever since I was a boy, one of my dreams was to qualify as a freefall parachute jumper. I thought it would be easy – but once I started my training I had to overcome the worst fear I've ever felt in my life - sheer terror.

Blue Peter viewers followed me every step of the way and they shared my total elation when I returned to San Diego in America and completed my training with the RAF Falcons.

It was a week I'll never forget as long as I live – a rollercoaster of every emotion – and I'm so happy I made it through. Whatever happens next, I've achieved a childhood dream.

Elizabeth B

Elizabeth was the daughter of King Henry VIII and Anne Boleyn. She was born at Greenwich Palace on 7th September 1533 and became Queen on the 17th November 1558 after the death of her sister, Mary.

Elizabeth ruled for 44 years and this period was called the Elizabethan Age – a time of great achievement and discovery which resulted in a huge empire.

My transformation from Elizabeth B., baker's daughter, to Elizabeth I, powerful Queen, began in studio 4 make-up. My hair was tied back and my face was covered with white make-up. My teeth were then coloured a revolting brown. There was no toothpaste in Elizabeth's day and as she was rather partial to sweet things, her teeth were soon rotten.

My hair was covered in what would have been a fashionable accessory - a curly red wig. Elizabeth owned over 80 wigs. The first layer of clothing was a chemise which looked like a long nightie. This was followed by stockings. Elizabeth loved silk ones which were tied with woollen cords.

Next came a corset which would have been stiffened with wood and iron and laced tightly at the back.

Blue Peter

As Elizabeth R

I felt incredibly regal as I walked around the studio and compared myself with Tussaud's waxwork model of Elizabeth.

Then the layering began - a petticoat, an overskirt, a farthingale (bum roll) which gave the dress its shape, a gown. Gowns often had separate sleeves and a bodice which would have been tied onto the skirt. Next, a winged collar and train followed by a ruff around the neck. This was a fashion from France and after the discovery of starch they became very elaborate items worn at the neck and wrists.

Finally jewellery. Queen Elizabeth had to dress more lavishly than anyone else at Court so was always weighed down with precious jewels. She was said to have had the most valuable collection in Europe and was one of the first to own a wrist watch.

Naturally Konnie and Simon rushed up to me bowing and scraping and asking if they could be of service. "Get me out of this!" I cried. The clothes were so heavy and I was incredibly hot. They helped me peel off the layers as quickly as they could but when I was down to my chemise, I had to cry out "Stop!" That was as far as they needed to go. Knickers hadn't been invented yet!

CRISPY

Where better to go to bake some delicious Christmas food than Hampton Court Palace which boasts one of the first complete Tudor kitchens ever built?

The fire was blazing in the hearth where 500 years ago there would have been huge joints of meat roasting over the flames. It was the perfect place to make my mouth-watering Crispy Mince Pies.

1 You will need two circular biscuit cutters – the 7 cm and 5 cm are ideal. Cut out a large and a small circle from each slice of bread.

It's a really easy recipe and the ingredients you will need are:

12 slices of medium white bread
12 teaspoons of mincemeat
50g butter
25g fine brown sugar

2 Melt the butter in a saucepan and lightly brush each large circle of bread coating both sides and around the edges. Push each circle into a bun tin to form the base of the mince pies. There is no need to grease the tin as the bread is already coated with butter.

MINCE PIES

3 Put a teaspoonful of mincemeat into the base of each pie.

4 Lightly brush the smaller bread circles with butter. Dip one side of each into fine brown sugar. Place each circle on top of the mincemeat, sugar side up.

5 Place the bun tin in the centre of the oven at gas mark 4 or 180 degrees Celsius for 10 to 15 minutes or until they have turned golden brown.

6 Empty the bun tray and place the mince pies on a cooling rack.

These mince pies are best eaten right away as they lose their crispness if stored.

43

SCRUM

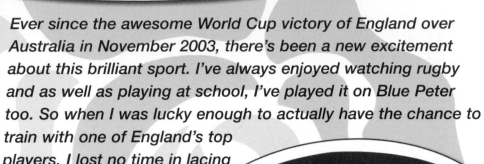

Ever since the awesome World Cup victory of England over Australia in November 2003, there's been a new excitement about this brilliant sport. I've always enjoyed watching rugby and as well as playing at school, I've played it on Blue Peter too. So when I was lucky enough to actually have the chance to train with one of England's top players, I lost no time in lacing up my boots and making my way to the home of English rugby – Twickenham stadium.

I was training with Will Greenwood, who played centre in that legendary World Cup win. I asked him how it felt when he realised England had won and he told me: "I jumped up and down with Wilko (Jonny Wilkinson) and we just shouted 'World Cup, World Cup, we've won it, we've won it!' over and over again!"

Many would say that victory in Sydney – and victory in any rugby match – depends on fitness and for the next 45 minutes I began to realise just how tough the training that goes into making a world-class rugby team really is. The session was designed to test our stamina and endurance to the limit and consisted of a series of pitch-length sprints, with Will passing the ball to me and vice versa. The focus was on maximum speed. Will has to be on the move throughout a game, side-stepping other players, so we also completed a shorter series of sprints using a course of cones to stand in for players.

In just a few minutes, my lungs felt as if they were bursting and an old leg injury had started to flare up. Usually at the end of any Blue Peter filming the director wants you to sum up how you're feeling – but by the end of the session for a few minutes, speech was beyond me. Will said it all – "That was hardcore".

DOWN!

Although rugby has traditionally been a men's game, increasingly women have started to take it up, too. The women's game is now so popular it even has its own Six Nations championships. I got the chance to play with the Harlequin ladies team and I soon discovered that all these ladies' took their rugby very seriously indeed.

"You don't mind getting knocked about a bit, do you, Liz?" asked Mel Antao, our team captain, with a smile.

I smiled back weakly. "Er, no…." It seemed the only polite thing to say – but it added to my nerves!

Our opponents were from Hove. I was playing on the wing and as soon as the match got started, I found myself in the thick of it. There was no time to be nervous any more and I just gave it everything I'd got. I managed to pass the ball at the right time. The time flew past and before I knew it the whistle had gone and the game was over. To my amazement and delight, the Harlequins had won. I was exhausted, covered in mud, with bruises that would last a good few days – but I'd had a brilliant time and a taste of why rugby is as much fun to play as it is to watch.

Blue Peter Flies

Copacabana Beach

Blue Peter

BRAZIL

Brazil in South America was the destination for our latest summer expedition. Home to 170 million people, it's the fifth largest nation on the planet and we started our trip in the city of Rio. Brazil is a Catholic country and the symbol of Rio is this 38-metre high statue of Christ the Redeemer situated right on top of Sugar Loaf Mountain. It's an awe-inspiring sight and Christ's open arms represent a big Brazilian welcome to all newcomers.

Rio also has two of the most famous beaches in the world – Copacabana and Ipanema – and we sampled the life led by the young beach crowd here – the cariocas. To be a true carioca, you must get the fashions right - girls wear skimpy bikinis and the boys tiny little swimming trunks. We'll leave you to decide whether you like the look or not!

Christ the Redeemer

The World!

After Rio we all split up to explore this massive country in more detail. Matt took a trip round the futuristic capital city, Brasilia, while Konnie went to a huge plantation where she followed the harvesting of coffee right from picking the beans or cherries to tasting the finished product (the knack is to sip, taste – then spit it out!).

Brasilia

Simon took an early morning boat trip in the wetlands of the Pantanal region in search of wildlife – and he found plenty of it. This is one of his snaps of a caiman, or small alligator – which got a bit too close for comfort.

Exploring the Pantanal

Coffee Tasting!

Matt and Liz teamed up to take a boat trip of their own – but theirs lasted a few days as they went to explore the wonders of the Amazon region. It is such a lush and exotic landscape – but as we discovered, it is under serious threat from developers. Let's hope something is done to protect all this natural beauty with its wealth of plants and wildlife before it is too late.

Up the Amazon

The Aerial View

Blue Pe

Dancing on the beach...

...was thirsty work!

Perhaps what will remind us all most of our expedition in the years to come is the rhythm of Brazil. This is a country where music is king and there's hardly a place where you don't stumble on music-making or dancing of some kind. Brazil is home to carnival – the festival which lasts days and features elaborate costumes. Matt went back to the beach for a lesson in samba – Brazil's favourite dance – from 11-year-old Luidy before taking part in the children's carnival. And we all had a go at making music Brazilian-style at the Grande Rio Samba School. You couldn't really hear our efforts as they were mostly drowned out by the noise being made by the professionals but even so, it was great fun to join in and have a go. And it's a fair bet that if you like music, colour, energy and life then you'll love Brazil as much as we did.

Carnival Time!

Blue Peter

The city on the water

Church on the Spilled Blood

ST. PETERSBURG

St Petersburg in Russia is one of the world's most beautiful cities. To mark its 300th birthday we ran a very special competition for a Blue Peter viewer to design an ornamental egg in the style of the fabulous Easter eggs made famous by Carl Fabergé, jeweller at the court of the Russian Tsar over 100 years ago. The winning design would be made into two real eggs by Carl Fabergé's great-granddaughter Sarah – one for the winner to keep, the other for the winner to present to the Peterhof Palace Museum in St Petersburg, where it would be kept on permanent display.

We received nearly 30,000 entries and it was a proud moment for our top prize-winner, 15-year-old Natalie Learmouth, when she saw her beautiful egg unveiled at the Palace for the very first time.

I took a trip on this canal

A very proud moment!

Time for inspection

While Natalie and her family took in the sights, I got stuck in – and joined the crew of the Aurora, the boat from which the first shots were fired in the bloody Russian revolution back in 1917. The Aurora is still a working ship today and I helped hose down her decks, soaking a few of the other sailors in the process!

One of my ship mates

Hosing duty!

The creepy Rasputin murder room

Echoes of the past are never far away in St Petersburg and I also went on the eerie trail of the mysterious Rasputin, the so-called Holy Man who became close friends with the last Tsar of Russia and his family. Rasputin was hated by almost everyone except the royal family and eventually he was murdered in this dingy cellar room. It has been carefully presented just as it was on that dark night, complete with wax effigies of the victim and his murderer. It was very creepy – maybe that's why I'm smiling in that rather fixed way!

And taking my bow!

That's me, flying high!

Before I left the city, I took up an invitation to take part in a traditional Russian dancing show in a huge theatre. After a bit of rehearsal, I was flattered and more than a bit nervous when I was given a key part in that night's performance. Nobody spoke a word of English but I was surrounded with warm smiles and gestures of encouragement. With the lights dazzling my eyes, I stepped on stage and danced as hard as I could before taking my bow in front of a packed audience - and I'm pleased to say that none of them spotted the imposter!

Blue Peter

On our way to the ranch

That's some horse box!

U.S.A

In the saddle, Wild West style!

Blue Peter

We've visited the United States a few times over the past few months but of course it's such an enormous country, we've barely scratched the surface!

I was lucky enough to go on two especially interesting trips. The first was to cowboy country – Wyoming in Colorado. Like a lot of people, I grew up with cowboy movies and I can't tell you how thrilling it was to rub shoulders with real-life cowboys and learn a little of their way of life. Liz and I stayed at a ranch and most days we were out on horseback. We even went on a Wild West cook out, washing down our grub with some good strong coffee. Yeehah!

For my next trip to the States, I was joined by Konnie as we set out to explore one of the Earth's most staggering sights – the Grand Canyon. The views looking over it really take your breath away – you feel about as big and important as an ant.

We had a chance to look up at the Canyon as well as down on it when we took a boat ride through the river which flows at the bottom. As well as crashing through some pretty choppy waters, we stopped long enough to attempt a spot of rock-climbing. It was thirsty work – but the views were worth every bead of sweat!

Sunset in the Grand Canyon

From the bottom looking up!

Ready to rock climb?

A trip we'll never forget...

Pet Draught

Transform an old fleece jumper into a cosy cat or dog draught excluder. They'll look cute all year round even when there isn't an icy blast blowing under the door.

You will need:

- an unwanted fleece jumper
- stuffing
- needle and thread
- coloured felt
- buttons
- a pipe cleaner
- a plastic milk bottle
- glue and wire bag ties

Excluders

1. Cut the sleeves off the fleece.

Turn one sleeve inside out and slide the other one inside so that the right sides of the fleece are facing each other.

2. To join the 2 sleeves sew around the cut edges using small running stitches. Oversew the last stitch and turn the sleeves to the right side. You will end up with a long tube shape.

3. Close one end by stitching all the way around the edge and pull the thread so the material gathers up. Oversew.

4. Fill the tube shape with stuffing and close up this end as before.

Blue Peter

5. For the head, cut out a circle from leftover fleece. A 26cm plate makes a good template. Sew small stitches around the edge of the circle and pull the thread to gather up the fabric. Leave a small hole and push in stuffing to shape the head. Pull the thread tight and oversew.

6. To make a cat, cut a nose and tongue shape from pink felt. For the muzzle and cheeks, draw a large shape from white or light coloured felt. Eyes can also be cut from felt or you could use buttons.

Cut 2 ear shapes from the fleece and 2 more in light coloured felt. Glue a wire bag tie down the centre of each fleece ear and then stick the felt ear shapes on top.

Position all the facial features on the head and when you are happy glue them in place.

For whiskers, cut 3 very thin strips from a plastic milk bottle. Thread each whisker onto a large eyed needle and push through the muzzle from one side of the nose to the other.

7. Stitch the head onto the body. Use a black marker pen to draw a line from the bottom of the nose to the top of the tongue.

8. From the leftover fleece cut a piece 30 cm long by 8 cm wide which will become the tail. Lay stuffing on one half of the tail and put a pipe cleaner on top. Roll to form the tail shape and stitch or glue in place. Fold one end into a point and glue or stitch. Attach the other end of the tail to the body and you will end up with a finished cat draught excluder.

9. If you want to make a dog – the muzzle is slightly different. Using a saucer as a pattern, cut out a circle from the fleece.

Cut the circle in half. You only need one half. Fold this in half, right sides facing, and sew the 2 straight edges together.

10. Turn the muzzle right sides out and fill the shape with a little stuffing. Sew or glue onto the head. Cut out a circle of black felt and cut a V shape from the edge to the centre. Pull the felt into a cone shape and carefully glue onto the end of the muzzle. The remaining features are the same as for the cat.

Blue **Peter**

ESCAPE FROM

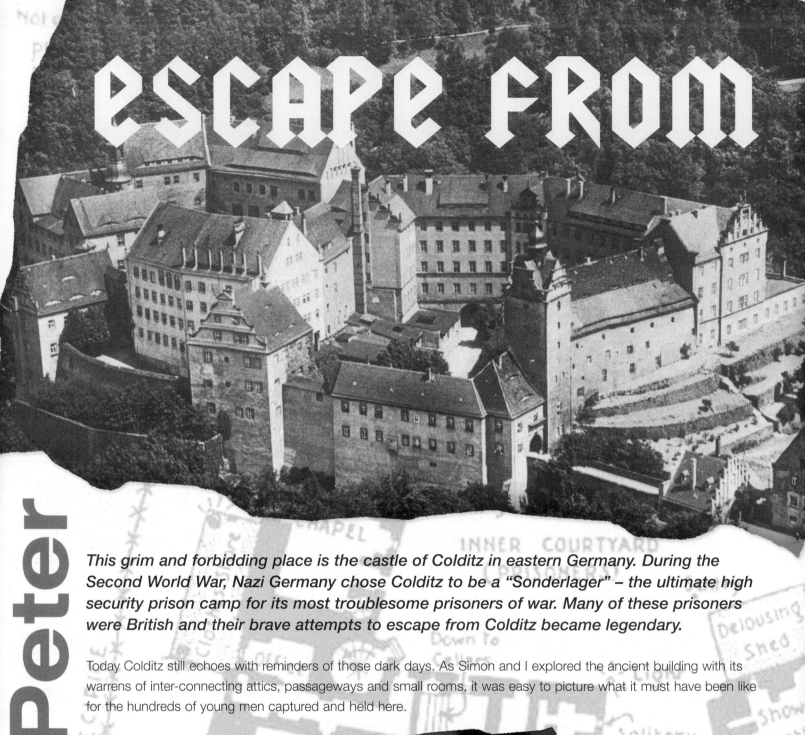

This grim and forbidding place is the castle of Colditz in eastern Germany. During the Second World War, Nazi Germany chose Colditz to be a "Sonderlager" – the ultimate high security prison camp for its most troublesome prisoners of war. Many of these prisoners were British and their brave attempts to escape from Colditz became legendary.

Today Colditz still echoes with reminders of those dark days. As Simon and I explored the ancient building with its warrens of inter-connecting attics, passageways and small rooms, it was easy to picture what it must have been like for the hundreds of young men captured and held here.

They had no way of knowing how long they would be kept here or if they would even leave alive. The only highlight was a precious letter or parcel from home. But they all knew their first duty was to try to escape.

COLDITZ

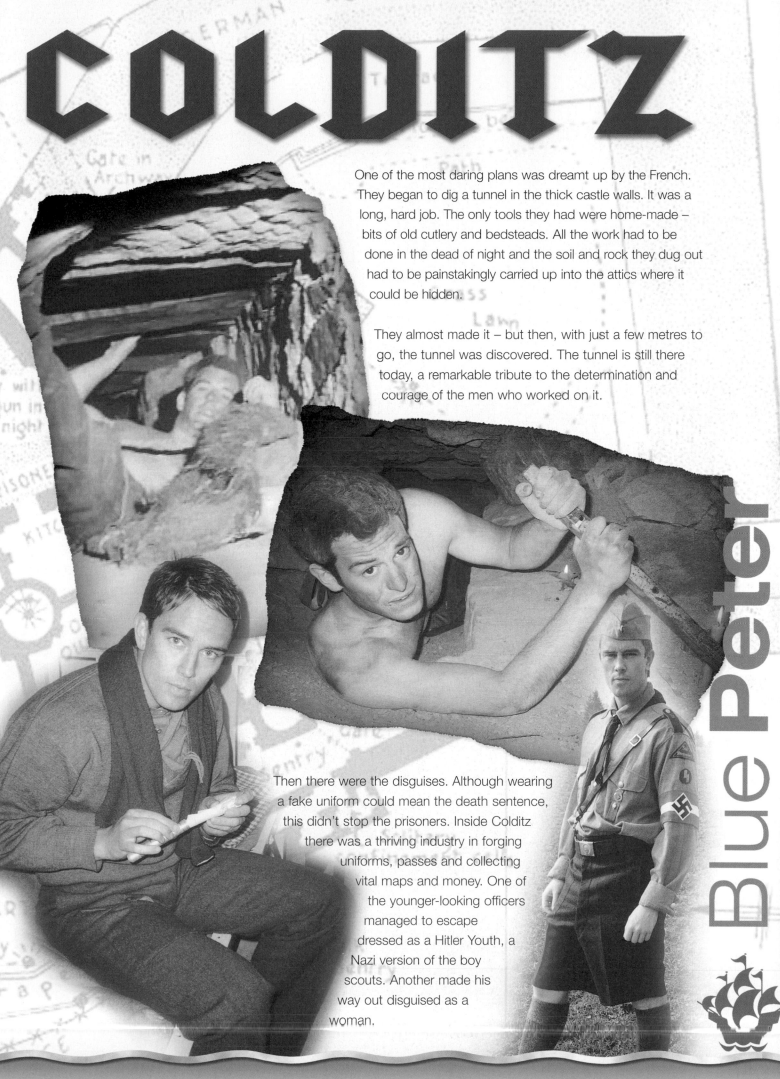

One of the most daring plans was dreamt up by the French. They began to dig a tunnel in the thick castle walls. It was a long, hard job. The only tools they had were home-made – bits of old cutlery and bedsteads. All the work had to be done in the dead of night and the soil and rock they dug out had to be painstakingly carried up into the attics where it could be hidden.

They almost made it – but then, with just a few metres to go, the tunnel was discovered. The tunnel is still there today, a remarkable tribute to the determination and courage of the men who worked on it.

Then there were the disguises. Although wearing a fake uniform could mean the death sentence, this didn't stop the prisoners. Inside Colditz there was a thriving industry in forging uniforms, passes and collecting vital maps and money. One of the younger-looking officers managed to escape dressed as a Hitler Youth, a Nazi version of the boy scouts. Another made his way out disguised as a woman.

Blue Peter

59

For every successful escape – and it's said that on average there was an escape attempt once every two weeks throughout the war - many failed. Recaptured men were punished with a spell in solitary confinement – but they never gave up hope. Despite the constant searches, the prisoners managed to keep in touch with the outside world using a radio. This was so well hidden, it was only uncovered during building work in 1993.

Blue Peter

Colditz was finally liberated on April 16th 1945. At long last, the remaining prisoners could go home. Back in the studio, Simon met one of them – 93- year-old Kenneth Lockwood – and awarded him our highest award - a gold Blue Peter badge - on behalf of all the prisoners kept in the castle. Mr Lockwood told Blue Peter viewers that his years in Colditz taught him the importance of tolerance – of getting on with people – and the value of freedom. As Mr Lockwood told his story, many of those watching on the studio floor felt tears in their eyes.

Today, although there is a small museum at Colditz, the castle is trying to forget the past. Slowly but surely, rooms are being ripped out, redecorated and altered beyond recognition. Graffiti left by the prisoners of war are being painted over. The plan is to turn the castle into a youth hostel.

Simon and I felt lucky to have had the chance to visit Colditz before it is transformed forever and to pay tribute to those prisoners of war who spent years there, plotting and dreaming of escape so that they could rejoin the fight for the freedom of their homes and families.

Blue Peter

Liz Barker

"I love being on Blue Peter. No day is ever the same and the programme has made me do stuff I'd NEVER in a million years have dreamt of attempting before I joined the team.

Check me out in my RAF flying kit, all ready to take part in the fearsome inverted spin – where the pilot deliberately lets the 'plane plummet towards the ground at high speed. Most people are sick the first time they experience it – I got through by shutting my eyes. Even without seeing the sky hurtle past, it was still one of the strangest sensations of my life.

Then there was the day in the studio where they told me I had to sing a duet with Simon for Children in Need. We rehearsed it all day long but only on the live programme did they reveal that my singing partner was actually going to be pop star Lemar. I just went for it and it turned out to be a lot of fun. It raised quite a bit of cash too!"

Blue Peter

Christmas

Blue Peter

Christmas comes just once a year but on Blue Peter we start planning our celebrations long before the big day. Out of over 120 Blue Peters a year, this is one of our favourites – partly because it gives us the chance to have a go at singing and dancing in some lavish production numbers.

We thought it would be brilliant fun to present a Blue Peter Christmas Songbook – our version of some of the most popular and best selling Christmas songs of all time. Although it would only last about 10 minutes on your screens, it took a lot longer than that to get ready. First, we had to record all our vocals to the special arrangements of the songs we'd chosen. As none of us could be described as natural singers, this was a challenge in itself! After that came a few days of rehearsing all our dance moves with our choreographer, Gary, who has worked with everyone from S Club and Westlife to the stars of Pop Idol. He has pretty high standards so shuffling about in the background and hoping not to be noticed wasn't an option!

is Coming

It took a whole day to record each number in our studio, with each one taking about 3 hours to set up, light, rehearse and perfect. It might sound like a lot – especially as each song was only around 2 minutes long – but with all the costume and wig changes, it took a marathon effort on everyone's part to get the job done. Each song had a different look and feel. We started with Mary's Boy Child, which has been a huge Christmas hit twice in the 1950s and 1970s. We went for a 70s hippy look with beads, flares and loads of hair.

Next was Frosty the Snowman – with Matt playing the snowman. It was all shot in a snowy scene but inside his Frosty costume, Baker was baking! "I reckon I lost a good few pounds in there – handy before all that Christmas over-eating!"

Then we recreated the 1970s glam rock look for our version of I Wish It Could be Christmas Every Day with Matt as the wild-looking lead singer in a pair of dangerously high platform boots. Simon played the drummer and we thought he looked as if he was auditioning for the Darkness!

Happy Christmas (War Is Over) has been a hit several times over. The set for this was our dream home – an ultra modern Blue Peter apartment – complete with Mabel, Lucy and Meg and a roaring fire!

The finale was another Christmas classic – White Christmas – given a Latin American spin. We got the idea from our expedition to Brazil and just like the carnivals there it was a riot of colour and energy. Liz found it very hard to see where she was going with all those feathers on her head!

A couple of weeks later, with our Songbook all edited together and ready to play in, we were rehearsing our live Christmas programme in Studio One at Television Centre – the biggest in Europe. And it was a good thing too because as well as cards, presents for the pets, a last-minute Christmas make and Blue Peter's Christmas crib we had to fit in over 300 children who were led, as always, into our studio by the Chalk Farm Band of the Salvation Army for the grand carol singing finale.

And as the last note of Hark! The Herald Angels faded away, we couldn't believe that after all the hard work and planning, it was all over for another year. Time to say our goodbyes and head off for Christmas with our families.

Hallowe'en

If you like parties, then Hallowe'en is a great excuse to invite some friends around. These hanging bats make a great decoration and at the end of the evening you can give them away as going home presents.

Blue Peter

Bats

Materials:

- A ping pong ball
- An old sock or dark coloured tights
- An elastic band
- A rectangle of material
- Needle and thread
- Ribbon, string or cord
- Small safety pin
- Card for templates
- Thin material like netting for the collar and wings
- Glitter pen
- Black felt for ears
- Coloured card or felt for eyes
- White card or felt for teeth
- Treats to fill the bat's body

1. The head is made from a ping pong ball. Cover it with a piece of sock or dark coloured tights. If the tights are thin, use double thickness to get good coverage.

Pull the ball into the middle and pull the material around it. Make sure it covers the ball smoothly and secure the bunched edges with an elastic band.

2. The bat's body is a rectangle of material. You could use another section from a thick pair of tights. Cut a piece roughly 30 x 20 cm and fold it in half lengthways. Thread a needle with matching thread and tie a knot in the end. Sew along one side with a running stitch, close to the cut edge. Finish the row of stitches about 1 cm from one end and oversew to stop them coming undone. Cut off the thread. Fold the material over to make 1cm hem and sew all the way around.

Blue Peter

69

3. Thread a length of thin ribbon, string or cord through this hem. If you attach a small safety pin to one end, you should be able to push it through quite easily. When it is threaded, take off the safety pin and tie the two ends together.

Turn the body right sides out. The end with the ribbon or cord will become the bottom of the bat's body.

At the top end, fold in a 1 cm hem and this time sew all the way around close to the fold rather than the cut edge. Do not cut off the thread but gently pull it so that the fabric gathers up.

4. Place the bat's head inside the gathers and tighten the thread until it fits snuggly. Use the long, leftover thread to sew the body firmly onto the head.

To hide any ugly stitches make a collar. You could make a ruff, a stand up collar or simply tie on a piece of ribbon.

5. The ruff is made from a long piece of material. Sew along one edge and pull the thread so that it gathers up and fits around the neck. Secure with one or two stitches.

6. For the bat's wings, draw a wing shape on a piece of card to make a template. Use this to cut two wings from thin material. A glitter pen daubed around the edges will make them sparkly. Sew or glue the wings on the body.

For the bat's face, cut 2 ear shapes from black material like felt which does not fray. Fold the bottom edge of the ear in half to give it a good shape and glue one on either side of the head.

The eyes are small circles of red or green with a black dot in the centre. The teeth are cut from white card or felt. Glue the features in place.

7. Fill the body with treats, pull up the ribbon and hang upside down until Hallowe'en.

Blue

Everyone loves a pizza so if you're having a party or simply thinking about treats for your packed lunch box, here are some tasty ideas.

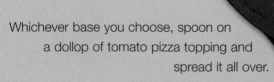
Pizza Toppings Ideas:

- sliced tomato and onion
- cheese feast (a mixture of cheeses)
- ham, mushroom and olives
- pineapple sweetcorn and tuna.
- chicken and peppers

Ingredients:

- ready cooked pizza base or for small pizzas try a sliced muffin
- tomato pizza topping
- cheese (mozzarella is the real thing but any grated cheese is ok)
- dried herbs (oregano or mixed)

Whichever base you choose, spoon on a dollop of tomato pizza topping and spread it all over.

Pizzas

Sprinkle on some herbs and then start dreaming up tasty toppings. Sliced fresh tomato, onion and cheese is always a winner. Or how about a cheese feast if you have a few varieties in the fridge? Ham and mushroom is a good combination as is tuna and sweetcorn.

Put muffin pizzas on a baking tray under a medium grill until the cheese starts to bubble – this takes around 5 minutes. If you are using a ready-made pizza base, follow the instructions on the packet.

Pizzas can be enjoyed piping hot or cold.

Blue Peter

Jaunie Vex

Blue Peter

Konnie Huq

"I can't believe this is my seventh year on Blue Peter – it has all gone so quickly. I think one of the reasons is that we're such good friends even though we're all very different. In fact, that's probably why it works so well. The boys can get a bit annoyed with Liz and me when we're deep in a chat or swapping ideas for tv shows and books we'd like to write or be in one day – but they always come round in the end!

Shortly after Simon and Matt had suffered 'P' Company (see pages 98-101), the Blue Peter film team decided to send Liz and me for a spot of P.E. in the mud with the Royal Marines. It was supposed to be a chance for us girls to show we could rough it too.

Now I was never a fan of P.E. at school – but this was far, far worse and performing press-ups and forward rolls in the thick, smelly mud of the River Exe was no joke. But when we got back to the studio and showed the film, you should have seen the size of Simon and Matt's smiles. Like I say, it's a good thing we're all friends!"

The Fool

This is me standing by all that's left of what was once one of Britain's most fabulous buildings, Fonthill Abbey. Its creator William Beckford lived just over 200 years ago and he was so rich he was known as "England's wealthiest son". This is his amazing story…

William was a very clever boy who studied hard and legend has it that his private piano tutor was the young musical genius, Wolfgang Amadeus Mozart.

When he grew up, he went travelling abroad in such lavish style people thought he must be an Emperor at the very least!

He celebrated his 21st birthday with a three-day-party. The most famous stage designer of the day created a fairy temple at his family home. William, who loved anything dramatic and stylish, was entranced!

His enormous wealth and his travels gave him the perfect chance to enjoy his favourite hobby – collecting. Books, furniture, paintings and ornaments – all of the very finest quality.

In France there had been a bloody revolution and as the rich and royal palaces were stripped of their fine contents, William was there to buy many of the choicest items for his collection.

On his return home, William shut himself away from the world. He planted a wood of one million trees to shield his home from public view.

A passionate animal lover, he built the Barrier – a seven-mile-long high wall topped with spikes to keep fox-hunters out of his land. His enemies nicknamed him "The fool of Fonthill".

Blue Peter

"Some people drink to forget unhappiness. I do not drink – I build!" said William and he began work on a new home, Fonthill Abbey, a magnificent building topped off with a colossal tower.

But he was impatient to get the building finished, it was a rush job – and the foundations were not strong enough. At night, alarming creaking noises could be heard throughout the Abbey.

"Fonthill Fever" swept Britain and everyone wanted to see it. But few were allowed in and William had man traps laid and specially trained bloodhounds to put off sightseers. Rumours about the strange, secret life he led inside the huge mansion kept him the talk of society.

Eventually William sold Fonthill – and just in time too. Just three years after he moved out, a deep groaning sound echoed through the countryside – and in one devastating moment of destruction, his magnificent tower collapsed.

After leaving Fonthill, William moved to Bath where he set about building another tower. "Higher!" he would command as it took shape, though it never matched Fonthill.

Building, designing, buying and hoarding, William Beckford, "England's wealthiest son", the "Fool of Fonthill," left a legacy of literally thousands of beautiful objects.

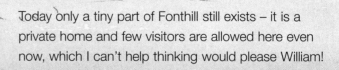

Today only a tiny part of Fonthill still exists – it is a private home and few visitors are allowed here even now, which I can't help thinking would please William!

His collecting mania never ceased and when he died in 1844, aged 84, he had been a leader of style for decades. I visited his grave, which is within view of the last home of Britain's greatest ever collector.

TOO HOT

For centuries martial artists have walked on hot coals and that was to be my hottest of challenges. But how would a novice like me do it?

Well, I at least had to look the part so it was on with a Gi which is the traditional martial arts suit. Step two was to join a karate class to learn some basic moves and loosen my body. I needed to start thinking (and breathing!) like a martial artist.

While I was indoors going through step three which was learning the correct breathing techniques – outdoors the fire pit had been dug and the coals lit. Pictures of fire filled my head but I had to concentrate on breathing out slowly and pulling in my stomach whilst making a sucking noise at the same time. When I had mastered the correct breathing technique, I had to learn to do it rapidly which left me feeling light-headed. This was exactly the desired sensation. My mind was flooded with oxygen which is a state known as being 'in the zone' - all the better for walking across white-hot coals without burning the soles of your feet.

Now for the walking part. I practised walking swiftly and I easily got into the correct stride. Next I had to walk with my eyes shut which was all part of the build-up to actually stepping out barefoot across white-hot coals.

Was I nervous? You bet I was. I started gabbling which was a sure sign of fear. I wasn't alone. A group of trainee martial artists had gathered outside around the fire pit. It was only 5 paces long but the heat was almost unbearable as we waited for the red coals to become even hotter and turn to white.

TO TROT!

Now it was my turn. Barefoot, I found the confidence to take up my position. Summoning all my willpower, I got ready for the challenge that lay ahead. Spencer called across the fiery divide, "look into my eyes". I stared hard. My eyes were boring into his. I heard his voice calling, "to me, to me, to me". Without looking down and almost without my knowing I put my right foot out and swiftly but steadily walked across hot coals.

As Spencer swept me into his arms when I reached the far side it seemed a miracle that I hadn't felt my feet burn. I had a good look and there wasn't even a blister! I felt very emotional and proud.

Scientists say that your feet aren't in contact with the hot coals for long enough to get burnt. However, without the help, encouragement and expert supervision I received from Bill and Spencer I'd never have plucked up the courage to do it!

P.S. Don't even THINK about trying this at home!!!

If you have a garden or balcony where you spend time on summer evenings, then these pretty lights will not only look decorative but ensure you can stay outdoors well after dusk.

Materials

- Empty jam jars and glass pudding basins
- Thick wire (florists' wire or fuse wire would be ideal)
- Coloured beads or rolled up scraps of foil
- Glass nuggets (optional)
- Tea lights

1. First of all you need to find some empty jam jars. See what pretty shaped jars and pots are just about to be emptied in your food cupboard or fridge and wash and dry them. Make sure that the neck of the jar is big enough to allow a tea light inside. If you can find a coloured glass jar it may not need any further decoration but you might like to paint your jar with special glass paint if you want a particular colour scheme.

2. A long handle is better and will give you scope to decorate it with beads. The handle is made from two lengths of wire. Florists' and fuse wire are ideal as they both bend and will curve around the neck of the jar. Place the jar in the centre of the wires and slowly twist them together on one side of the neck.

3. Now split the two wires so that they wrap around the neck of the jar and twist the ends, keeping going between each side until the wires fit very snugly around the rim in between the grooves that the lid was screwed onto.

Lights

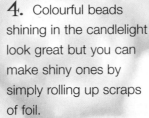

4. Colourful beads shining in the candlelight look great but you can make shiny ones by simply rolling up scraps of foil.

5. Thread some beads onto both sides of the jar but leave roughly 30 centimetres at the end of each length of wire.

6. Pull the two ends together to form a handle and use up any spare wire by twisting it into a small loop.

7. You will have loads of ideas for decorating your garden lights. Glass nuggets or glitter glue work beautifully. Then all you need is a tea light and somewhere safe to hang it outdoors.

Use a long taper to light the tea light but always check with a grown-up before doing so. Garden lights are a perfect way to prolong a summer evening and in the morning you can replace the tea light for another occasion.

Blue Peter

ON THE

Once upon a time, boxing was a sport most parents approved of and boys who boxed were thought of as brave and heroic. It is a sport with a long and bloody history and because of the violence involved and a few high-profile deaths and injuries, today boxing has become a very controversial sport indeed. Yet it is still watched and played throughout Britain, films about boxing are as popular as ever and boxers like the great Mohammed Ali are among our national heroes.

I set off to Wales to spend the day with Britain's best boxer, Joe Calzaghe, who first made his name in 1997 when he beat champion Chris Eubank to become the WBO super middleweight champion. He's not lost a fight since.

BluePeter

ROPES

For a champion, Joe turned out to be a quietly spoken and modest man, though there wasn't much time to chat when I first arrived because it was a training day. Joe was preparing for his next big fight and nothing, not even a day's filming with Blue Peter, could interrupt the hard graft. As I wanted to get some idea of just how fit you need to be as boxer, I joined Joe as he set off for a demanding run.

The running helps build stamina, a big heart and big lungs – vital for a boxer like Joe who may have to slug it out for twelve rounds. After the run, it was off to the gym. I couldn't help but be impressed with Joe's focus, his strength and speed. While he was working, he was truly a different man – nothing could distract him from putting one hundred per cent into each task.

I asked him why he boxes.

"I fight because I want to win. I also fight to be financially secure – I will retire in two or three years. I want to go down as one of the best fighters to come out of Britain. When I was a kid you played football or you boxed. Now boxing is a dying sport. There are a lot of other things kids can do these days."

When I said that I didn't think Joe looked like a boxer, he laughed: "The ones that don't look like the boxers are the good ones because they don't get hit."

Joe has two sons and I wondered if he would encourage his boys to get involved in boxing: "I think it is good exercise, it teaches self-discipline. But I wouldn't advise them to take it up seriously. There are other sports to do. They could make it in tennis, football, golf."

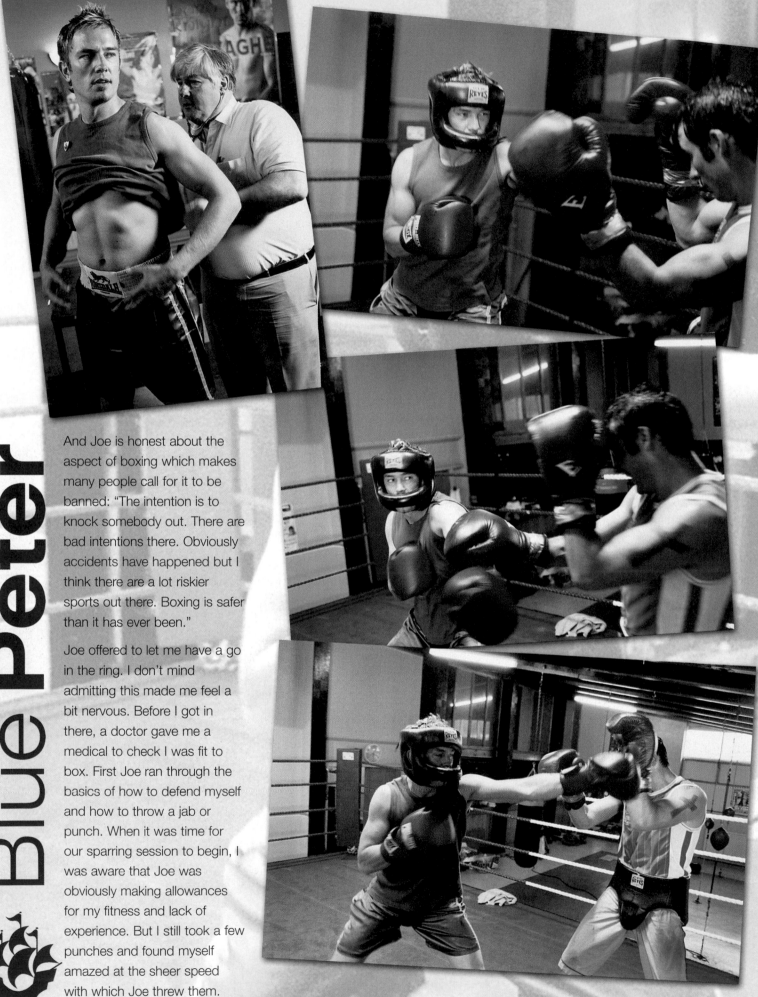

Blue Peter

And Joe is honest about the aspect of boxing which makes many people call for it to be banned: "The intention is to knock somebody out. There are bad intentions there. Obviously accidents have happened but I think there are a lot riskier sports out there. Boxing is safer than it has ever been."

Joe offered to let me have a go in the ring. I don't mind admitting this made me feel a bit nervous. Before I got in there, a doctor gave me a medical to check I was fit to box. First Joe ran through the basics of how to defend myself and how to throw a jab or punch. When it was time for our sparring session to begin, I was aware that Joe was obviously making allowances for my fitness and lack of experience. But I still took a few punches and found myself amazed at the sheer speed with which Joe threw them.

When we'd finished, I was exhausted and as Joe had to leave for his annual brain-scan, something required from all professional boxers, I thought that was it. I was wrong! Joe's dad, Enzo, offered to give me one last training session and it's one I'll never forget as long as I live. Sessions of fifty sit-ups and press-ups at a time, at a relentless pace, and I lost it. I just couldn't go on. "Now you know the level of fitness boxing demands", Enzo smiled grimly.

To me, Joe looked more like a film star than a boxer – but there was no mistaking his formidable ability in the ring and out of it. It had been eye-opening to see him in action, close-up – and I'd really enjoyed meeting him. But I left Wales still unsure what I felt about boxing itself – on the one hand, you can't deny the heroism, skill and sheer stamina involved – but neither can you ignore the violence and aggression required. If Joe is right and boxing does die out in Britain, he will be one of the last British champions in a sport which can trace its origins back through hundreds of years.

Blue Peter

Matt **Baker**

"Another Blue Peter year has rushed past and I think what I like most is the variety – there really is no other programme like it. I'm sure that when I'm old and grey, I'll get out all my Blue Peter annuals, pore over the pictures and remember some of the happiest days of my life.

Some of my magic memories from this year are of the incredible people I've filmed with – like Rugby World Cup hero, Jonny Wilkinson, who I met when he trained the winners of our Blue Peter Rugby competition. Jonny is already a legend – but he's also one of the nicest blokes I've ever met.

Other highlights were the few days I spent with the cast of the world-famous Holiday on Ice – it was a great feeling to glide along as part of their spectacular show, though I'm still not sure about my costume! I'm even less sure about what I wore, or rather didn't wear, when I came face to face with British sumo wrestling champion Steve Paton. Despite my best efforts, I was soon on the studio floor, gazing up at the lights.

Then there was the unforgettable week when I invited the 72-year-old nomad Ali Louche (who I'd met on our summer trip to Morocco) back to Britain to stay on my family's farm. Although he spoke no English and I didn't speak his language, we got on like a house on fire – even when he offered to kill one of our sheep for dinner!

Lederhosen

We do loads of dressing up on Blue Peter but I think that one of the most bizarre dressing-up assignments Matt and I have ever faced was when we were invited to join a traditional Austrian dance group with a unique dress code – lederhosen – which, roughly translated, means leather shorts.

Lederhosen have a long and fascinating history – they have been traditional dress for boys and men in both Austria and Germany for hundreds of years, rather like the kilt in Scotland.

Before Matt and I could meet up to face our dancing challenge, it was my job to track down the lederhosen we would actually wear for our performance. My investigations led me to a strange shop called Lederhosen Wahnsinn – which means Lederhosen Madness – and the man who runs it, Herbert Lipah. He calls himself the King of Lederhosen and after a few minutes' chatting, I could quite see why. His shop was crammed to the rafters with thousands of pairs and all the accessories – braces, belts, shoes and thick socks.

His Majesty told me that lederhosen were invented by farmers – often made from deer or cow skin – and they were really practical for an outdoor life, cool in summer and warm in winter. I was amazed to discover that one second-hand pair can cost hundreds of pounds and this is because lederhosen are often passed from father to son through many generations. The older they are, the more prized they become.

Madness

I'd thought that selecting the right lederhosen would be easy but there were so many different kinds, I didn't know where to begin. His Majesty said the easiest thing would be for me to borrow a few pairs to find out which I liked best and that's just what I did. Lederhosen are actually very comfortable and I soon discovered that although you'd stick out like a sore thumb walking about dressed like this in Britain, over here no-one batted an eyelid – except to give me the occasional compliment!

After my truly bizarre modelling assignment, I made my choices and set off to meet up with Matt in the mountain town of Soell. All dressed up and raring to go, we arrived for rehearsals with the local lederhosen dancing group. We were to perform an ancient woodchopping dance and the idea was to make the crowd laugh. Dancing in lederhosen involves lots of slapping – of both your thighs and backside – and those of the other dancers – so never mind making the crowd laugh, we were soon in hysterics.

That night in front of a packed audience, we took to the stage in all our finery and gave the Dance of the Funny Woodchoppers our best shot. It was a great laugh, the crowd seemed to love it and although it was one of the strangest things we've ever done, I must admit that Matt and I wouldn't have missed it for the world!

Easter

Who'd have thought these gorgeous Easter Bunnies are made from an old pair of socks? They make great presents which will last a lot longer than chocolate eggs!

Materials

- pair of socks
- matching sewing thread
- polyester stuffing or cut-up tights
- ready-made fluffy tail or cotton wool ball
- thread for whiskers
- felt or paper for eyes and nose
- stiff cardboard for feet
- elastic band
- ribbon for bow
- glue

Bunnies

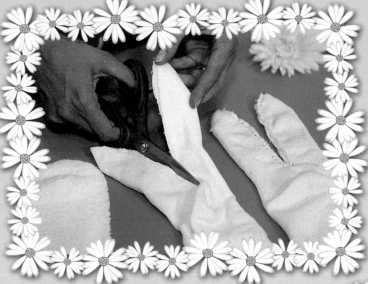

The first thing you have to do is form a long pair of ears. They are made form the toe end of one sock. Turn the sock inside out and flatten it so that the sole faces upwards and cut down the middle of the sock from the point of the toe to about two-thirds of the way to the heel.

Now sew the cut edges together to form the ears. You don't need to be an expert at sewing. Just sew small, straight stitches which will sink into the sock material hiding any occasional crooked ones.

Next, turn the sock the right side out and stuff the head and body. You can use polyester stuffing or cut-up tights.

When the body and head are stuffed to the right size cut off any spare sock material at the bottom. The actual amount you need to cut off will depend on the length of the sock.

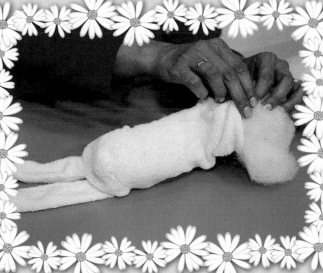

Turn under a small hem at the bottom edge and sew straight stitches through the hem all the way round, then pull up the thread tightly to gather the sock material and close up the opening. Oversew the last stitch a few times.

Tie a thread round the base of each ear and knot firmly to form a perfect pair of floppy ears.

Wind an elastic band around the neck and mould the head and body into shape.

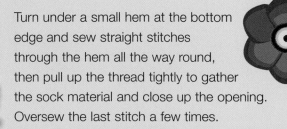

The feet are cut from the toe end of the second sock. They need stiffening so that the rabbit will stand properly. First draw and cut out a foot pattern from thin card. Draw around this pattern twice on stiff card and cut out the foot shapes.

Cut off the toe section from the sock making sure that it is long enough to cover the length of the foot. Cut the toe section in half lengthways. Fold one piece in half with the right sides together and stitch the side edges together.

Put some glue on the flat ends of the feet and place the body firmly in place over the glue.

The front legs are made from oblong pieces cut from any straight part of the remains of the sock. Fold in half with the right side inside and sew the open edges together along one end and the long side. Turn right side out and stuff. Sew and gather up the open end in the same way as for the body. Glue both legs in place on the rabbit body.

The whiskers are made by tying several lengths of thread together in the middle. The nose is a small circle of felt. Put glue on one side of the nose then press in place on the rabbit's face with the middle of the whiskers underneath.

The eyes are circles of felt but coloured paper works just as well. Glue a small dark circle onto a lighter one then glue in place.

You can buy a ready-made pompom for a tail or use a cotton wool ball. If you give a cotton wool ball a squirt of hairspray it will make it stay in shape. Finish off with a bow of ribbon tied around the Easter bunny's neck.

The egg baskets are made from yoghurt pots or cheese spread containers.

Blue Peter

95

BATH

People have been coming to Bath for over 2000 years and when Simon and I visited the city we did a bit of time-travelling to find out why.

Our first stop was at the city's Roman baths. The Romans were big fans of water. They called Bath Aqua Sulis and they built a great pool to make the most of the healing waters here – which must have been a great comfort to them, stuck as they were in a cold and hostile country many miles from the warmth of their own homes back in Italy. These remarkably well preserved ruins were only uncovered around 120 years ago and they're well worth a visit.

After the Romans left Bath, it was many years before the healing waters became fashionable again. Then around 300 years ago fashionable people began to flock here once more to 'take the waters'. You can still 'take the waters' today in the city's elegant Pump Room. Several glasses are recommended for maximum benefits – but to be honest, one glass each was enough for Simon and me!

SPA

The fashion for 'taking the waters' shaped the beautiful city you see today with its grand squares and crescents built from the famous honey-coloured Bath stone. One house in the imposing Royal Crescent has been kept just as it would have been in its heyday. I took tea as a fine lady of the time and it was easy to see why a holiday or season in Bath, full of dances and gossip, would have been a highlight of the year. As the famous writer Jane Austen, who was a regular visitor here, once wrote – "Oh who can ever be tired of Bath?".

While I was trying my hardest to act like a proper lady, Simon dressed up as Beau Nash - the man who led high society here – and he was surprised to discover that Nash even drew up a series of rules to show people what they should wear and how they should behave.

Much of Bath would still be recognised by Beau Nash today and I think he and his fashionable friends would be delighted to know that a multi-million-pound new Spa centre has just been opened where people can enjoy themselves by bathing, relaxing and having all kinds of 21st-century treatments in the very same hot bubbling water which has been the secret of the city's success for thousands of years.

THE PAIN OF

Most of the time, the Blue Peter production team relies on our general fitness to get us through all the action and sport we cover on the programme. But when our boss told us that for this assignment we'd need three months of training in the gym beforehand, we knew we were really in for it.

Blue Peter

The training certainly helped but to be honest, nothing can really prepare you for the sheer physical intensity of the week-long 'P' Company. The 'P' stands for Pegasus, the winged horse from Greek mythology who was the first airborne warrior. For the men who undergo it, 'P' Company is a series of gruelling tests you must pass before you can get a job with the army's elite airborne services. As the officer in charge told us with a grim smile: "Pain is only temporary. Failure lasts a lifetime!"

For us, there wasn't a job at stake - but this would be the ultimate test of our fitness.

'P' COMPANY

First we had to pass the pre-selection tests. These included circuit training in the gym, a daunting 8-mile speed march, and a 6-mile run. They all passed in a haze of pain. We got through – but only just and it was a shock to discover that despite the training we'd put in, by the standards of 'P' Company our endurance was weak. It is hard to describe how bleak it feels to be given low marks when you've really tried your best. But the men who run the course are tough and they weren't making exceptions for a couple of blokes off the telly.

The next day was known as Black Thursday and that's because of two races dreaded by all the men who undertake them. First up was the log race – 1.8 miles of pure hell. In the race, each team carries a 60-kilo log between them. No one is allowed to hold the race up and if you falter, they pull you out. The best way of describing the muscle-ripping, joint-jarring agony you go through is that you simply enter another dimension – neither of us was aware of the Blue Peter cameras filming our every step.

Legs like jelly, hearts pounding – we so wanted to make it. But it wasn't to be. Once we'd stumbled, we were both pulled out. Words couldn't express our disappointment and, besides nothing we said made much sense, we were so out of it.

Like the log race, the stretcher race is a legend throughout the army. It's a 4-mile run with teams of up to 16 carrying a 60-kilo metal stretcher. Everyone takes a turn to carry the stretcher for about a couple of minutes at a time and believe us – a couple of minutes is about as much as anyone can take.

Work hard, focus, keep going – we were determined to make a go of it – and we did. We both completed the course through a blur of blood, sweat and mud. Once our lungs had stopped burning, we shared a bottle of water between us – and it tasted like nectar!

When it was all over, the training staff congratulated us both on the effort we'd put in – and these are not men in the business of handing out false praise. Afterwards, aching and exhausted on our way back to London, we talked about what we'd gone through – how seriously hard you need to be to pass 'P' Company – and how until the week we tried it, we didn't really know what pain was.

Let's Get

If your dolls are in need of a good workout then they'll be pushed to the max in this fully equipped gym in a box.

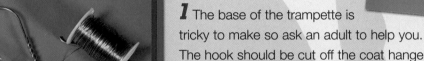

The Trampette is made from:

- round cheese box
- wire coat hanger opened out or similar wire
- black tights or sock
- thin elastic
- silver leatherette fabric

1 The base of the trampette is tricky to make so ask an adult to help you.
The hook should be cut off the coat hanger and pliers used to form 4 legs around an 8 cm square. A short length of fuse wire wrapped around the ends will hold the frame in place.

2 Push the whole cheese box into the foot of a sock. Cut off the excess and sew up the open end.

3 Cut a strip of silver fabric 38 x 7cm. Join the short seam with small running stitches. Make a small hem on both of the long edges. Thread some thin elastic through both hems, pull and fasten off. Fit around the edge of the circular box.

4 Fasten the trampette to the frame with a few stitches around each leg.

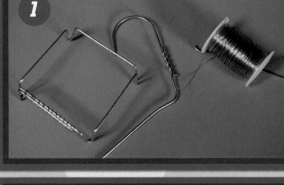

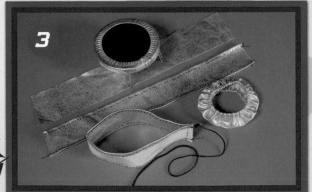

Physical

The Punch bag is made from:

- insulating foam tube
- length of chain
- fabric to cover
- modelling clay
- thin card
- lolly sticks

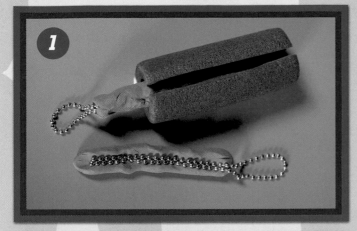

1 Cut a length of chain 32 cm long. Cut a 10 cm length of tube. Cut a circle of thin card using the circumference of the tube as a template. Open out the tube and fill with modelling clay. Fold the chain in half and press onto the modelling clay.

2 Cut a circle of fabric 1 cm larger than the card circle and glue the card to the wrong side of the fabric. Snip the extra fabric around the circle – turn over and glue the snipped bits to the back of the card. Glue this to the bottom of the tube.

Cut a rectangle of fabric big enough to cover the tube. Stitch a hem along one long edge leaving the thread attached. Cover the tube with the fabric gathering at top and fasten around chain.

Blue Peter

3 To support the punch bag on the wall of the gym you'll need 4 lolly sticks painted silver to look like reinforced steel.

4 Glue 3 of the sticks together with the middle one sticking out about 2 cm. Make a small groove on the fourth stick. The punch bag will hang in this groove so it doesn't swing off. This stick needs to be attached to the wall at a right angle. Use a pencil to lightly mark where you want to position it. Make a small slit with a craft knife and push the stick in place. Make a second slit in the wall roughly 7 cm below the first and push the triple stick through it. Glue the other end in place.

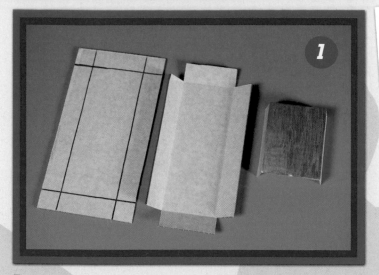

The Treadmill is made from:

- corrugated cardboard + extra
- 2 silver straws
- 4 black straws
- 2 cotton reels (long thin ones) – painted silver
- plastic air freshener container – painted silver
- silver fabric
- stiff card + sticker shapes
- fabric for runner

1 Cut out a rectangle from corrugated cardboard 23 x 12 cm. Mark and score lines 2.5 cm inside all around. Cut out the corners and bend the sides up. Tape together to form an open box and paint it silver.

Pull the front off a plastic air freshener container and trim around the front edge of the back section so that it fits snugly in the 4.5cm gap at one end of the box. Have the empty side facing the box. Paint silver – leave to dry.

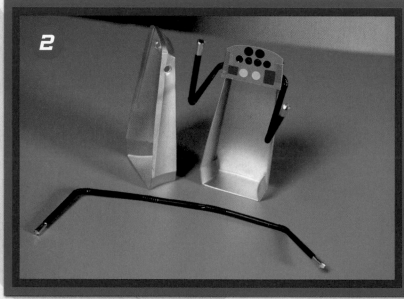

2 Make holes in each side at the top of the container big enough to push a straw through. Join 4 black bendy straws together to form handle bars. Cover the ends with silver tape.

Use the top of the container as a pattern to cut out a piece of card which will become the control panel. Paint it silver and stick on some coloured sticker shapes. When the treadmill has been completed this can be taped to the top of the container.

Cut 2 lengths of silver straw each 10 cm long. Cut small grooves in the box big enough for straws to sit in, two at 2 cm from one end of the box and the other two about 4.5cm from the other end.

Cut a piece of card to fit inside the box between the 2 grooves. Cut a second piece of thin card the same length but wider so that when these flaps are bent the support will sit in the box.

3 For the running band cut a strip of fabric about 30 x 4.5 cm and join the short ends.

Thread the straws through the cotton reels then through the running band. Do the same at the other end and then slip the support inside before placing inside the box. Place the control section in the remaining gap and the treadmill is finished.

Blue Peter

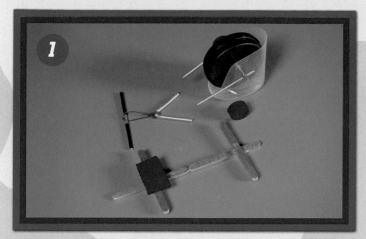

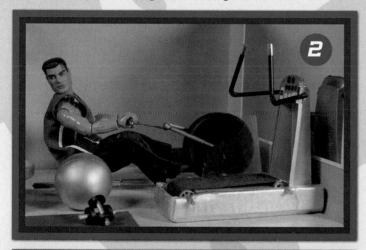

The Rowing Machine is made from:

- lolly sticks
- handlebars: straw & tape
- 2 large lids
- seat: card, foam, fabric
- plastic bottle with square base
- pedals: card, black foam
- string or elastic band
- thin dowelling

1 Make a hole through the centre of both large lids and both small ones. Glue the large ones together.

Mark and cut the plastic bottle so that the lids fit. It should be about 10cm at the back. Make holes in each side and push a 10 cm length of dowel through one side of the bottle – through both lids – and through the other side of the bottle. The lids should NOT touch the bottom or the back of bottle.

Join another 10 cm length of dowel each side of the lids and use thin wire to join. Push the small lids on to the axle to cover the wire join.

To join the upright sticks at the top – cut a length of straw so that you have 5 cm each side of the bendy part. Stretch out the bendy part and glue the straight bits over the sticks.

Tie some string or loop an elastic band through the bendy bit of straw.

Stick 2 lots of triple lolly stick together and join these also so that you have one long stick.

Make 2 lots of legs by glueing 3 lolly sticks together on top of each other.

Glue these legs to the underside of the long stick. 3.5 cm from the front and 5.5cm from the back.

2 To make the rowing machine seat cut a piece of thick card 5 x3 cm. Glue a piece of foam on top and then cover with fabric or sticky backed plastic. Glue this to the top of long stick on top of the back leg.

Finally make a HANDLEBAR using a 12 cm length of thin dowelling. Wrap black tape around each end and loop the other end of the elastic band over the centre. Slot the ends through your doll's hands.

3 Finish off your dolls' gym with lots of accessories. We made a big mirror from silver card.

The dumbbells are simply thin dowelling pushed onto black tap washers.

The gym ball is a plastic ball painted silver. The mats are cut from coloured foam sheets – ours measured 18 x 8 cm.

Skipping ropes are lengths of coloured cord and plasma screens are just thick card painted silver with small pictures stuck on the front.

We're sure you'll have lots of ideas of your own. As all the best trainers say "No pain, no gain!"

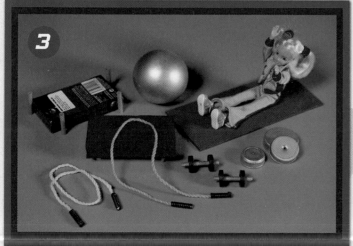

Blue Peter

Goodbye George, Hello Shelley

April 28th and a 'phone call came through to the Blue Peter office with the sad news that dear old George the tortoise had died quite suddenly. Our friend Marina, who looked after him, had taken George to the vet after he developed breathing problems but there was nothing the vet could do. Experts think he was around 83 years old and that he simply died of old age.

Remembering George

George had been on the programme almost 22 years to the day – and in that time he'd been friends with 20 presenters as well as millions of Blue Peter viewers. We knew he was popular but we were astonished by the reaction to the news – which even made the front page of the world-famous Times newspaper!

We buried George in the place he loved best – the Blue Peter garden – on May 10th, with a special plaque and a Blue Peter rhododendron bush to mark the place.

Konnie welcomes Shelley to the team

Many journalists wanted to know if we'd have another tortoise on the programme – but our viewers already knew the answer to that. Just a few weeks earlier, we'd introduced a 15-year-old Mediterranean spur-thighed tortoise (the same breed as George) as a friend for George. Blue Peter viewers named her Shelley and although it is sad that she didn't know George for long, we hope that Shelley (who is already making a name for herself as the speediest tortoise we've ever seen!) will be with us for many years to come.

Hello Shelley

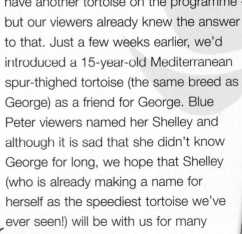

Blue Peter

Win a Day With Blue Peter

How would you like to visit the Blue Peter studio? Meet the presenters, have your photo taken with them and get their autographs? Pat the pets and visit the Blue Peter garden and go home with a bag full of Blue Peter goodies?

If the answer is yes – then why not enter our competition?

The winner, with friend and family (maximum of four persons) will be able to spend the day with us and the winner's transport costs to the studio will be provided. Photographs will be taken of the day and will feature in next year's annual.

How many Girl Guides?

This is what you have to do. Study this photograph carefully. It was taken on the day we crammed our studio with the Hampshire West Girl Guides. But exactly how many of them were there? Once you've decided on a number, simply send your answer, along with your name, age and address to:

Blue Peter Day Out
CBBC
Television Centre
London
W12 6BP

Competition entries must be received by 28th February 2005. Visit date will then be agreed with the winner, who will be notified by post no later than 30th April 2005.

RULES
1. Entrants must be under 16.
2. One winner will be chosen from the correct entries at random and notified by post.
3. The judges' decision will be final and no correspondence can be entered into.
4. A list of winners will be made available on request from Pedigree after 31st January 2005. Please enclose an S.A.E.
5. Employees (and their relatives) of Pedigree and the BBC are not eligible to enter
6. Entries are limited to one per person.
7. The competition is open to residents of the UK, Ireland and the Channel Islands.
8. The publishers reserve the right to vary the prizes, subject to availability

Blue Peter

Blue **Peter Badges...**

...*are special because we don't just give them away. There are five different badges and here's how you can win one.*

BLUE badges are what the presenters wear. You could win one by sending an interesting letter, a good idea for the programme, a story or a poem.

SILVER badges are awarded to viewers who have already won a Blue badge.

GREEN badges are our environmental awards. If you tell us about an environmental project or give us your views about any 'green' subject, you could win a Green badge. Let us know how you are helping the world around you.

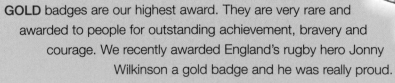

COMPETITION badges are awarded to winners and runners up. We love running competitions and there are always lots of runners-up as well as winners.

GOLD badges are our highest award. They are very rare and awarded to people for outstanding achievement, bravery and courage. We recently awarded England's rugby hero Jonny Wilkinson a gold badge and he was really proud.

Solutions & Credits

Our address is:
Blue Peter
BBC TV Centre,
London W12 7RJ

Our home page is:
http://www.bbc.co.uk/cbbc
E-mail: bluepeter@bbc.co.uk

Written by Richard Marson and Anne Dixon

All makes by Gillian Shearing except Tracy Island and Easter Bunnies by Margaret Parnell

Food by Phil Haynes

The Fool of Fonthill illustrated by Bob Broomfield

Photography by Chris Capstick

Other photographs by:
Matt Baker, Jon Hancock, Adrian Homeshaw, Kez Margrie, Richard Marson, Ross Millard, Mark Pinder, Simon Thomas, Shirin Smith, Sue Osmond, Richard Kendal

Cover photographed by:
BBC/Richard Kendal

If we have left anyone out, we are sorry!

The authors would like to thank the whole Blue Peter Team for their help and ideas. Every effort has been made to contact copyright holders for permission to reproduce material in this book. If any material has been included without permission, please contact us.

Solutions for Hello There!

1. and 2. The Queen of Mean – we all loved going back to the 60s to battle the evil time slider Kismet Stryker in our Quest adventure serial.

3. and 4. Recognise us? We got dressed up for a special Euro Peter, celebrating the catchy songs and silly dance routines that make the Eurovision Song Contest such a laugh.

5. Blue Peter Editor Richard Marson and Series Producer Kez Margrie with the team and the two BAFTA awards won by Matt and the programme.

6. Menaced by monsters from the eerie world of time traveller Dr Who.

7. Konnie gets cosy with Titanic director James Cameron. Mabel Goes To Hollywood anyone?

8. Pass the spot cream! I've died a few times on Blue Peter. This time it was all part of the sad story of Eyam village, where plague killed hundreds of its people. Simon even managed to shed a real tear over my death scene!

9. A dance group with a difference. To celebrate 40 years of Top of the Pops we invited a group of famous CBBC female faces to become Peter's People – our tribute to the days before pop videos when Top of the Pops had its own all-girl dance group called Pan's People who gyrated to the latest hits when an artist couldn't make it to the studio.

10. 12-year-old Ryan Gilpin, presenter for the day after winning our 45th birthday competition.

11. Top group Girls Aloud as you've never seen them before – or since – on the day they became models for our look at the history of nurses' uniforms over the years.